AI and the Project Manager

Enabling project managers to adapt to the new technology of artificial intelligence, this first comprehensive book on the topic discusses how AI will reinvent the project world and allow project managers to focus on people.

Studies show that by 2030, 80 percent of project management tasks, such as data collection, reporting, and predictive analysis, will be carried out by AI in a consistent and efficient manner. This book sets out to explore what this will mean for project managers around the world and equips them to embrace this technological advantage for greater project success.

Filled with insights and examples from tech providers and project experts, this book is an invaluable resource for PMO leaders, change executives, project managers, programme managers, and portfolio managers. Anyone who is part of the global community of change and project leadership needs to accept and understand the fast-approaching AI technology, and this book shows how to use it to their advantage.

Peter Taylor is a project management expert, speaker, author, and consultant. He is also a change expert who has built and led five global PMOs across several industries and has advised many other organisations on transformation strategy. He is the author of the Amazon number one bestselling project management book *The Lazy Project Manager*, along with many other books on project leadership, project marketing, project challenges, and executive sponsorship. In the last few years, he has delivered over 450 lectures around the world, in over 25 countries.

AI and the Project Manager

How the Rise of Artificial Intelligence Will Change Your World

Peter Taylor

NEW YORK AND LONDON

First published 2022
by Routledge
605 Third Avenue, New York, NY 10158

and by Routledge
2 Park Square, Milton Park, Abingdon, Oxon OX14 4RN

Routledge is an imprint of the Taylor & Francis Group, an informa business

© 2022 Peter Taylor

The right of Peter Taylor to be identified as author of this work has been asserted by him in accordance with sections 77 and 78 of the Copyright, Designs and Patents Act 1988.

All rights reserved. No part of this book may be reprinted or reproduced or utilised in any form or by any electronic, mechanical, or other means, now known or hereafter invented, including photocopying and recording, or in any information storage or retrieval system, without permission in writing from the publishers.

Trademark notice: Product or corporate names may be trademarks or registered trademarks, and are used only for identification and explanation without intent to infringe.

Library of Congress Cataloging-in-Publication Data
Names: Taylor, Peter, 1957– author.
Title: AI and the project manager : how the rise of artificial intelligence will change your world / Peter Taylor.
Description: New York, NY : Routledge, 2022. | Includes bibliographical references and index.
Subjects: LCSH: Project management–Technological innovations. | Artificial intelligence–Industrial applications.
Classification: LCC HD69.P75 T3889 2022 (print) | LCC HD69.P75 (ebook) | DDC 658.4/04–dc23
LC record available at https://lccn.loc.gov/2021020166
LC ebook record available at https://lccn.loc.gov/2021020167

ISBN: 978-1-032-00656-7 (hbk)
ISBN: 978-1-032-00657-4 (pbk)
ISBN: 978-1-003-17506-3 (ebk)

DOI: 10.4324/9781003175063

Typeset in Sabon
by Newgen Publishing UK

To Juliet Taylor, love you totally. Peter

To the memory of Carolyn Lambert, my wife of 54 years. Everything I have accomplished in project management was made possible through her love and unwavering support! Lee

Contents

About the Author	*xii*
Acknowledgements	*xiii*
Foreword by Antonio Nieto-Rodriguez	*xiv*
Introduction	*xix*

1 What This Book Is (and Isn't) — 1

2 Background — 5
Artificial Intelligence 101 5
Why AI and Why Now? 7

3 The Rise of the Machine — 11
Myths and Legends 11
First Beginnings and Winters 12
High Points from Fantasy to Reality 12

4 Categories of AI — 17
Process Automation 17
Chatbots 17
Machine Learning 18
The Autonomous Project Manager 18
Is It AI? 19
How Much Data? 20

5 Explainable AI — 25
A Question of Trust and Reliability 26
So, What Is Explainable AI? 27
Don't Expect to Comprehend the Unexplainable 29
We Are Only Human After All 32
Augmented Actionable Insight 33

x Contents

6 People-centric AI   41
Don't Be a Hater! 41
AI Isn't AI, and You Don't Always Need It Anyway 42
AI-fuelled Coaching of Leaders and Teams 45
Project Matching 46
Prediction 47
Market Predictions in Project Management 48
Project Success Measurement 48
Chatbots for People/Automate Communication Intelligently 49
How Do We Use AI? Understanding Root Cause in Project Failure 50
The Boring but Important: Data Privacy and Ethics 50
Conclusion: People-centric AI 51

7 Resistance Is Futile   55
Don't Be a Vogon 55
Your Virtual Partner 58
But You Need to Change That Mindset 60

8 Projects Are About People   63
Three Big Asks 63
Project Team Analytics 64
The Opportunity of AI 65
Perfect Symbiosis 66

9 AI and the Lazy Project Manager   71
Keep It Simple 71
Going for an AI Drive 72
Keep On Being 'Lazy' 74

10 A Perspective from the Old and the Wise   77
Illusion Confusion 77
Actionable Information 78
No Free Lunch 79
Beneficial Uses of AI in Project Management 80
Some Serious Considerations 83
What Won't AI Do for Project Management? 84

11 A Perspective from the Young and Enthusiastic   87
Hope and Fear! 87
Digital Natives 88
Smart People Need Smart Tools 89
Science Fiction to Science Reality 90
The Data Jungle 91
The AI Marketplace 91

Automated Tasks May Not Be AI in Action 93
What Excites Me? 93
Concluding Thoughts 94

12 Thoughts on the Future Project Manager   99
Five Big (as Yet) Unanswered Questions 99
In the AI/PM World, Can Anyone 'Do' Project Management? 100
In the AI/PM World, Will Certifications Be Valueless? 100
In the AI/PM World, Will We Abandon Methodology? 103
In the AI/PM World, Are Professional Bodies Irrelevant? 104
In the AI/PM World, Will Our Skills Be Devalued? 104
Much to Ponder 105

13 Survey   109
Introduction 109
AI in Project Management: Survey Response Details 109
Personal Thoughts 117

14 A Final Word: Fish Have Hands   122

15 Other Weird and Interesting Facts   125

My Valued Contributors   *127*
I'll Be Back   *133*
Index   *134*

About the Author

Peter Taylor

Keynote speaker, consultant, trainer, and coach, Peter is the author of the number one bestselling project-management book *The Lazy Project Manager*, along with many other books on project management, PMO development, executive sponsorship, transformation leadership, and speaking skills. His many books published in the last 11 years include:

- *Project Management: It's All Bollocks*
- *Make Your Business Agile: A Roadmap for Transforming Your Management and Adapting to the 'New Normal'*

Peter has delivered over 450 lectures around the world in 25 countries and has been described as 'perhaps the most entertaining and inspiring speaker in the project management world today'.

He is a passionate believer in the power of people in project management, continuous change, and the world of the business agile.

www.thelazyprojectmanager.com

Acknowledgements

As with any book, thanks need to go to many people.

I will specifically thank all of my contributors to the book chapters as and when we 'meet' them on the following pages. I would like to thank the respondents to my survey on artificial intelligence. The *Thoughts from the Real World* sections in the book include some of their responses; full quotes can be found in the 'Survey' chapter.

For now, I will thank Meredith Norwich, Senior Editor at Taylor & Francis/Routledge, for championing my book proposal for 'AI and the Project Manager' (and a second one at the same as it happens on project teams, brave lady), along with all of the production staff at Routledge who have made this book as good as it can be.

I will also thank the team at PMI Germany for commissioning a workshop on 'AI: The End of Project Management as We Know It' back in 2020, which further fuelled my understanding and passion for this specific topic, as did my work with Nikki Horwood and the team at Sharktower prior to that, contributing to their Mighty Notes book, *Will AI Change the Way You Manage Change? Seven Project Management Experts on How People and Data Can Work Together for Better Outcomes.*

And a last, sarcastic, acknowledgement to the global pandemic for giving me all the time I needed to research and write this book. I could have done it without you, but it would have taken a bit longer.

Foreword by Antonio Nieto-Rodriguez

2021 and beyond... Disruptive Trends in Project Management

In the next five years, the world will see more projects than ever. The reconstruction of the economy, healthcare, social care, and society at large after the devastating COVID-19 global pandemic crisis will be unprecedented in human history. According to McKinsey,[1] in just the first two months of the crisis, governments announced $10 trillion in reconstruction funds, which is three times more than the response to the 2008–09 financial crisis. These are millions of projects, which will need millions of project managers.

2021 is going to be the confirmation of the 'Project Economy', a term I conceived in 2018 when working on my earlier book, *The Project Revolution: How to Succeed in a Project Driven World*.

However, despite this positive outlook, significant trends will put at stake the project management profession that we have learned to know in the past 40 years. We should consider these signals as an urgent call for profound change in our practices and a much-needed change in our competencies. A small price to pay compared to the unique opportunity that the project management profession has to lead what I call our new world driven by change.

Today, about 70 percent of projects fail to deliver their objectives. What if we commit to doing much better? If we increase our success ratio from 30 percent to 60 percent, we would be adding approximately the GDP of China in benefits, impact, value, and social good.

These are the five most important trends I see for 2021 and beyond:

1. The End of Job Descriptions, the Start of Project Roles: The move from a world driven by efficiency to a world driven by change will have enormous consequences in terms of strategies, culture, organisational structure, competencies, compensations, etc. More and

more work will be carried out through projects. The Richards Group is the largest independently owned ad agency in the US, with billings of $1.28 billion, a revenue of $170 million, and more than 650 employees. Stan Richards,[2] its founder and CEO, removed almost all of its management layers and job titles, leaving only that of the project manager. The Richards Group is not an exception. One of the most significant impacts of this unprecedented disruption will be the end of job descriptions, which almost every organisation has had for the past 30 years; these will be replaced by project roles. Today, most employees don't work on what their job descriptions state; they work on changing priorities, strategic initiatives, a focus on the clients, and delivering value to their organisations. They actually work on projects. Employees very soon will be assigned a role in a project, and once the project is over, they will be assigned a role in another project.

2. From Project Manager to Strategy Implementation Professionals: It's about the competencies to succeed in the Project Economy. My own research for the current book I am writing, the *HBR Project Management Handbook*,[3] clearly shows that senior leaders see project management as a core competency and plan to invest in project managers over 2021 and beyond. However, project managers will need to learn new skills, and evolve to become what I call strategy implementation specialists. They will need to start working on the project earlier on, within the innovation phase, facilitating ideation and using design-thinking techniques to ensure that the best ideas are chosen and developed into products that generate value through the right project management approaches. With the slow absorption of project management tasks by AI (see trend #5), most manual tasks will be replaced by leadership, strategic, and value creation competencies. The main challenge was that before, there was no course to help project managers, scrum masters, and managers to make this step change in their careers. I am proud to say that over the past two years, I developed the first global online course and certification as part of the Strategy Implementation Institute.

3. Expanding Our Toolkit, It Is Not a Waterfall or Agile; It Is Both and More: Many of us grew in our careers by developing and implementing project management methodologies with the idea that one size fits all – meaning that all projects need to follow the same methodology, the same project life cycle, the same templates... In the 1980s, 1990s, and 2000s, the focus was on traditional waterfall methods; in the 2010s, it moved to Agile; all projects then had to follow an agile approach. Today, we know that this is wrong; you cannot have just one method to address all the projects and changes you have in your organisation. In 2021, we will see the evolution

of implementing projects into a set of tools, which will include agile practices, traditional project management practices, and some design thinking, innovation, lean start-up, programme management, and change management. Depending on the type of project, project managers should be able to apply one tool or different techniques simultaneously.
4. The Project Management Office: Evolve or Game Over: The second big trend is the end of the PMOs as we have known them for about 40 years. During this period, PMOs were set up as a group in a hierarchical structure, either reporting to the CIO, CFO, or the CEO. However, hierarchies are structures of the past; today, most organisations look for more agile settings, with fewer management layers, promoting project-based work and self-managed teams. Therefore, PMOs need to change urgently. I see two essential evolutions. First, PMOs should move to cover strategy and transform into strategy implementation offices. Second, we need to develop agile PMOs, temporary entities that will assist in traditional and agile projects. Once the project is over, the PMO should transition into running, operating, or selling what the project has produced and delivered.
5. And finally, the subject of this very book, artificial intelligence, and its impact on project management. In my view, AI will, without any doubt, disrupt project management; sooner than we expect. According to Gartner, 80 percent of project management tasks will be taken over by AI by 2030.[4] Today, most projects are still managed with Microsoft Project, software launched in 1987, more than 30 years ago. Project portfolio management tools offer more advanced features, but are far from being applications benefitting from the latest technologies. Based on personal research, in 2021, we will start seeing some algorithms that can predict the success rates of projects, validate the projects' scope, and automatically design a project plan in a few minutes.

These changes, some of them incredibly significant, will impact and even disrupt the role of the project manager. Project managers will need to embrace AI and take advantage of these new technologies to increase project success. We currently think of cross-functional project teams as a group of individuals, but what if we may soon refer to them as a blend of humans and robots? The project leadership, the project manager of the future, will need to develop strong soft skills, leadership, strategic thinking, business acumen, and good understanding about technology.

Some organisations are already building AI into educational and certification programmes. Northeastern University is incorporating AI into its project management curriculum,[5] teaching project managers how to use AI to automate and improve data sets and optimise investment value from projects.

None of this means that human project managers will be going away; on the contrary, the role of the project manager will likely be more important than ever, though the scope will change. We can expect a similar impact of AI and automation to professionals in operations, sales, finance, etc.: a shift from tactical to strategic. For project managers, that means that while AI and automation are completing administrative work, the project manager's focus will be on ensuring that project results deliver the expected benefits and are aligned with strategic goals.

Losing a significant part of our current tasks as project managers might be scary for many; I see it as a vast opportunity to switch our focus to more added-value activities and drive an increase in project success ratios.

Finally, I want to share a global challenge and new aspiration for our project management community for 2021. Today, about 70 percent of projects fail to deliver their objectives. We urgently need to step up and significantly increase the project success rate. Considering that every year approximately $48 trillion US dollars are invested in projects, we fail to deliver trillions of benefits, value, and impact in organisations and society at large. It is colossal, unbearable, and embarrassing. What if we commit to doing much better? If we increase our success ratio from 30 percent to 60 percent ? Just imagine the amount of value that we would be adding to the world: approximately the GDP of China in extra benefit. Imagine if we do that not only in 2021 but year after year. The Project Economy is here. The world needs top project managers more than ever. But we need to reinvent project management, embrace AI, adapt, and grow fast. Let's not waste this unique opportunity!

> There are fewer 'low-cost' ways of working more inclusive, impactful, motivating and inspiring than being part of a project with an ambitious goal, a higher purpose, and a clear fixed deadline.
>
> (Antonio Nieto-Rodriguez[6])

Notes

1 Ziyad Cassim, Borko Handjiski, Jörg Schubert, and Yassir Zouaoui, 'The $10 trillion rescue: How governments can deliver impact'. McKinsey & Company, 5 June 2020. www.mckinsey.com/industries/public-and-social-sector/our-insights/the-10-trillion-dollar-rescue-how-governments-can-deliver-impact

2 Burt Helm, 'Stan Richards's unique management style'. *Inc.*, November 2011. www.inc.com/magazine/201111/stan-richards-unique-management-style.html.

3 Antonio Nieto-Rodriguez, *Harvard Business Review Project Management Handbook: How to Launch, Lead, and Sponsor Successful Projects*. Harvard

Business Review Press, 2021. www.amazon.co.uk/Harvard-Business-Project-Management-Handbook-ebook/dp/B08LHGKBKY

4 Gartner, 'Gartner says 80 percent of today's project management tasks will be eliminated by 2030 as artificial intelligence takes over'. Press release, 20 March 2019. www.gartner.com/en/newsroom/press-releases/2019-03-20-gartner-says-80-percent-of-today-s-project-management

5 Mary Ludden, 'What impact will artificial intelligence have on project management?' Northeastern University graduate blog, 10 January 2019. www.northeastern.edu/graduate/blog/ai-and-project-management/

6 Antonio Nieto-Rodriguez is a World Champion in Project Management; Thinkers50 & Top 30 Global Gurus; PMI Past Chair; Professor; HBR Author; Founder, Strategy Implementation Institute; Founder, Projects & Co; Director, PMO; Marshall Goldsmith Executive.

Introduction

AI (artificial intelligence) will reinvent project, programme, and portfolio management.

A bold statement, I realise, but it is not one that I alone believe in.

Gartner states that by 2030 – so we are not talking too far ahead – 80 percent of the work of today's project managers will be eliminated as AI takes on functions such as data collection, tracking, reporting, analytics, and predictive analysis.[1]

80 percent of what you do as project managers today – or what your project managers do if you are head of a PMO or head of a programme, or project practice – 80 percent of that work will just not be there anymore; it will be eliminated because AI will take it on, and deal with it, and deal with it no doubt in a very consistent and better manner.

This book explores what that means for project managers around the world and how good project managers will embrace this technological advantage for greater project success.

The Core Messages:

> AI will reinvent your project world, but it will allow you to focus on the people, and projects are about people.
> The project management world needs to understand what is coming at them at speed – and that is AI.
> Learn, adopt, adapt, or fall behind, and inevitably fail.
> An AI-empowered project management future is a good thing.

All project 'people' need to think 'AI' now and in the future. AI is one of the most important steps up in terms of how humans will interact with the planet, with each other, and with technology that we've had in our lifetime. It is a true game-changer. A paradigm shift.

AI is more than just a buzzword in business; it's more than just headlines or articles in magazines and on TV and social media; it's more than some nerdy niche technology.

In this book, I aim to not just introduce you to the technology that is AI (from a very broad perspective I have to be honest, just to give you a view of the AI landscape you understand), nor just to the business and strategy aspects of AI, but also to cover the particularly important ethical, societal, and legal aspects of AI as well as exploring the impact of AI on my profession, project management.

The increasing use in AI is coming, whether you like it or not, and you will have to learn to engage with it or say 'goodbye' to the project world as it leaves you trailing behind.

Note

1 Gartner, 'Gartner says 80 percent of today's project management tasks will be eliminated by 2030 as artificial intelligence takes over'. Press release, 20 March 2019. www.gartner.com/en/newsroom/press-releases/2019-03-20-gartner-says-80-percent-of-today-s-project-management

Thoughts from the Real World:

'Project Management definitely needs Intelligence. Be it Natural or Artificial'.

Chapter 1

What This Book Is (and Isn't)

It is important, I think, for you to understand what this book is, and what this book isn't.

Let us start with what it isn't.

It is not a deep technical book on AI architecture or programming or anything like that; that is way beyond my understanding, and it would be shameful of me to even suggest I could talk about it – I can't.

There are many other books out there that can go into that kind of depth if that is what you really want. Here are some of the books I used to research the topic:

Author	Title	Year
Paul Boudreau[1]	*How the Project Management Office Can Use Artificial Intelligence to Improve the Bottom Line* – independently published	2020
Paul Boudreau	*Applying Artificial Intelligence to Project Management* – independently published	2019
David Brown[2]	*Artificial Intelligence for Business: Understand Neural Networks and Machine Learning for Robotics. A Step-By-Step Method to Develop AI and ML Projects for Business* – independently published	2019
Igor Luzhanskiy and Anastasiia Kyryliuk[3]	*The Guide to AI Chatbot Project Management* – self-published	2019
Ray Kurzweil[4]	*The Age of Spiritual Machines: When Computers Exceed Human Intelligence* – Viking Press	1998

DOI: 10.4324/9781003175063-1

2 What This Book Is (and Isn't)

There are also many online articles, and you will find references/links to all of these in the endnotes of each chapter.

So, what *is* this book?

Well, I hope it is an opportunity to see practical insights into what is out there with regard to AI in project management. Now.

To also understand what is coming. Soon.

And finally, to understand the 'what if' scenario of the future.

Once you have that understanding, I hope that it also gives you some kind of inspiration with regard to professional project management. I hope that is thought challenging for you. I hope it inspires you about what could be and what possible changes you need to make in your 'perhaps' mindset and your approach to project management.

I also hope, as with all of my books, that it is written at a consumable level; that is, it is reasonably easy to understand, and it is reasonably comprehensive in its scope to allow you to walk away, having finished the book, with an understanding of AI in the project management world.

And, if I am successful in that aim, I must also thank my valued contributors, who have helped make this book what it is through the provision of real insights from current tech providers in the marketplace, and real project managers, from either end of the career spectrum. All of which sits alongside my own personal thoughts, insights, and understanding of AI in the project management arena.

The project management world needs to understand what is coming at them at speed – and that is AI.

At present, in this rapidly moving subject, I believe there is no comprehensive book that talks about project management and AI at the people level, and no book that hears what the technology providers are planning for us project managers – trust me, they are hyper-excited about what is possible now and what is going to be possible in the coming months – and no book that asks the really important questions about the future of project management and everything that surrounds and feeds/feeds off this still evolving profession.

As such, this book will be unique and the first real AI in project management book on the market from an authoritative publishing house.

It was an absolute pleasure to write this book and I look forward to hearing from my readers your thoughts on AI, on project management, and on this book.

Notes

1 Paul Boudreau: Professor, speaker, project manager – Greater Ottawa Metropolitan Area. www.linkedin.com/in/boudreaupaul/
2 David Brown, *Artificial Intelligence for Business: Understand Neural Networks and Machine Learning for Robotics. A Step-By-Step Method to*

Develop AI and ML Projects for Business, 2019. www.amazon.com/Artificial-Intelligence-Business-Step-Step-ebook/dp/B0829S494Q
3 Igor Luzhanskiy and Anastasiia Kyryliuk, *The Guide to AI Chatbot Project Management*, 2019. www.amazon.co.uk/Guide-AI-Chatbot-Project-Management-ebook/dp/B07X7HTY21
4 Raymond Kurzweil is an American inventor and futurist. He has written books on health, AI, transhumanism, technological singularity, and futurism. Kurzweil is a public advocate for the futurist and transhumanist movements and gives public talks to share his optimistic outlook on life extension technologies and the future of nanotechnology, robotics, and biotechnology.

Thoughts from the Real World:

> 'Like any improvement there will be twists and turns before it is seen as useful, usual, and then we will wonder how we ever managed without it'.

> 'Project management is a dying need in most organisations, so AI is either irrelevant or the replacement to project management'.

Chapter 2

Background

AI is a field of computer science dedicated to solving problems which otherwise require human intelligence, but with the assumed objective of both freeing up human effort and also carrying out such solutions with greater efficiency.

Artificial Intelligence 101

> Artificial Intelligence is the designing and building of intelligent agents that receives percepts from the environment and takes actions that affect that environment.[1]

In some ways, AI is not new; well, at least it is not a 'new' concept.

The term 'artificial intelligence' was coined by John McCarthy,[2] a Stanford University professor, in 1955. The Turing test, originally called the imitation game by Alan Turing in 1950, is a test defined to assess a machine's ability to exhibit intelligent behaviour equivalent to, or indistinguishable from, that of a human.

The most common association that people have with AI is either the T-1000 from *Terminator 2*[3] or HAL 9000 from the classic film *2001: A Space Odyssey*,[4] which is a less than welcoming or positive attitude. But even the 'experts' are not wholly convinced, it seems, with Stephen Hawking[5] suggesting that AI could go either way: it will be 'either the best, or the worst thing, ever to happen to humanity. We do not yet know which'.[6]

At a very high level, AI can be categorised into two broad types: narrow (weak) AI and general (strong) AI.

Artificial narrow intelligence (ANI), also known as 'Weak' AI, is the sort of AI that exists in our world today – whether it is organising personal and business calendars, being able to play chess, or analysing data to produce reports. Siri,[7] Cortana,[8] Alexa,[9] and Google Assistant[10] are all examples of narrow AI.

DOI: 10.4324/9781003175063-2

Artificial general intelligence (AGI), or 'Strong' AI, refers to machines that exhibit human or adaptable intelligence. This is the sort of AI that we see in movies, such as the ones mentioned above. AI experts are fiercely divided over how soon it will become a reality. As such there are no real-world examples of general AI.

What other terms will you come across? Well, here a few of the obvious ones:

- Machine Learning (ML)
    - This is the study of computer algorithms that improve automatically through experience.
- Applied Intelligence
    - This is a faster and more effective approach to collecting, processing, and analysing (lots of) data, creating insights which help identify clear opportunities to act on, and automating, those actions where possible to unlock business value.
- Deep Learning
    - This is a subfield of machine learning concerned with algorithms, inspired by the structure and function of the brain called artificial neural networks.
- Responsible AI
    - This is a framework that focuses on ensuring the ethical, transparent, and accountable use of AI technologies in a manner consistent with user expectations, organisational values, and societal laws and norms.
- Predictive Analytics
    - This encompasses a variety of statistical techniques from data mining, predictive modelling, and machine learning that analyse current and historical facts to make predictions about future events.
- Computer Vision
    - This is an interdisciplinary scientific field that deals with how computers can gain high-level understanding from digital images or videos.
- Natural Language Processing (NLP)
    - This is a psychological approach that involves analysing strategies used by successful individuals and applying them to reach a personal goal. It relates thoughts, language, and patterns of behaviour learned through experience to specific outcomes.
- Intelligent Automation
    - This combines robotic process automation (RPA) with artificial intelligence (AI) to automate complex business processes using AI robots.

- Dark Data
    o This is data which is acquired through various computer network operations but not used in any manner to derive insights or for decision making. The ability of an organisation to collect data can exceed the throughput at which it can analyse the data.

There is a great series of videos called 'What Is Artificial Intelligence, Really?' from Accenture[11] that talks in more detail about each of these – go check it out.

Why AI and Why Now?

Dr. Athina Kaniouram[12] stated that 'Artificial Intelligence (AI)... is shaping up to be the single biggest technology revolution the world has ever seen. It's a completely new factor... capable of driving business growth by augmenting natural human expertise, taking automation to new places, and diffusing innovation throughout society'.[13]

She further stated that:

> AI technologies are finally hitting the mainstream. Thanks to the combinatorial effect of today's unprecedented levels of technology innovation in so many different fields, today's AI applications can make use of virtually unlimited cloud processing, exponentially faster custom-designed chips, and ever greater levels of computational efficiency.

According to Gartner,[14] by 2020, AI will generate 2.3 million jobs, exceeding the 1.8 million that it will remove – generating $2.9 trillion in business value by 2021.

Google's CEO[15] goes so far as to say that 'AI is one of the most important things humanity is working on. It is more profound than... electricity or fire'.[16]

Ron Schmelzer, in an article for *Forbes*, stated:

> AI, with its unique ability to monitor patterns, is a capable assistant to project managers. Studies have shown that project managers spend more than half of their time on administrative tasks such as dealing with check-ins and managing updates. AI bots are capable of stepping up and handling these less intensive tasks for the project manager with current systems cutting time spent on busywork in half.[17]

Regarding project management Sunil Prashara, ex-President and CEO at the Project Management Institute, stated: 'Our world is undergoing massive disruption. From COVID-19 to equality movements to AI going mainstream, tectonic shifts are causing upheaval and shaping the future. Project professionals are well-positioned to turn these challenges into positive change.'[18]

I can keep these coming thick and fast, but so that you can progress to the more interesting part of the book just consider the following:

> AI is here, and more is coming.
> AI will deliver a seismic impact over the next few years.
> We will all be affected in some way(s).

It is equally scary and exciting, depending upon your viewpoint, but (as we will learn later in this book), resistance will be useless.

Notes

1 Stuart Russell and Peter Norvig, *Artificial Intelligence: A Modern Approach*. Pearson, 2009.
2 John McCarthy was an American computer scientist and cognitive scientist. McCarthy was one of the founders of the discipline of artificial intelligence.
3 *Terminator 2: Judgment Day* (also promoted as T2) is a 1991 American science fiction action film produced and directed by James Cameron.
4 *2001: A Space Odyssey* is a 1968 epic science fiction film by Stanley Kubrick. The film, which follows a voyage to Jupiter with the sentient computer HAL after the discovery of an alien monolith affecting human evolution, deals with themes of existentialism, human evolution, technology, artificial intelligence, and the possibility of extraterrestrial life.
5 Stephen Hawking was an English theoretical physicist, cosmologist, and author who was director of research at the Centre for Theoretical Cosmology at the University of Cambridge at the time of his death in 2018.
6 University of Cambridge, ' "The best or worst thing to happen to humanity" – Stephen Hawking launches Centre for the Future of Intelligence'. Research news, 19 October 2016. www.cam.ac.uk/research/news/the-best-or-worst-thing-to-happen-to-humanity-stephen-hawking-launches-centre-for-the-future-of
7 Siri is a virtual assistant that is part of Apple Inc.'s iOS, iPadOS, watchOS, macOS, and tvOS operating systems.
8 Cortana is a virtual assistant developed by Microsoft which uses the Bing search engine to perform tasks such as setting reminders and answering questions for the user.
9 Amazon Alexa is a virtual assistant AI technology developed by Amazon.
10 Google Assistant is an AI-powered virtual assistant developed by Google that is primarily available on mobile and smart home devices.
11 Accenture, 'What is artificial intelligence, really?' [Video series]. www.accenture.com/gb-en/services/digital/what-artificial-intelligence-really?

12 Dr. Athina Kaniouram – Chief Strategy and Transformation Officer at PepsiCo. www.linkedin.com/in/dr-athina-kanioura-6176077
13 Accenture, 'What is artificial intelligence?' www.accenture.com/us-en/insights/artificial-intelligence-summary-index
14 Gartner, 'Gartner says by 2020, artificial intelligence will create more jobs than it eliminates'. Press release, 13 December 2017. www.gartner.com/en/newsroom/press-releases/2017-12-13-gartner-says-by-2020-artificial-intelligence-will-create-more-jobs-than-it-eliminates
15 Pichai Sundararajan, known as Sundar Pichai, is the chief executive officer of Alphabet Inc. and its subsidiary Google.
16 Catherine Clifford, 'Google CEO: A.I. is more important than fire or electricity'. CNBC, 1 February 2018. www.cnbc.com/2018/02/01/google-ceo-sundar-pichai-ai-is-more-important-than-fire-electricity.html
17 Ron Schmelzer, 'AI in project management'. *Forbes*, 30 July 2019. www.forbes.com/sites/cognitiveworld/2019/07/30/ai-in-project-management
18 PMI, 'Megatrends 2021' report. www.pmi.org/learning/thought-leadership/megatrends

Thoughts from the Real World:

'The right practitioner will use AI as a tool to predict outcomes, select the team, and execute the human activities that deliver results'.

'Some companies are still so confused on project management... cumbersome and technical debt stand in the way of use of AI'.

Chapter 3

The Rise of the Machine

Myths and Legends

The history of AI began, arguably, in antiquity, with myths, stories, and rumours of artificial beings endowed with intelligence or consciousness by master craftsmen.

Thousands of years before machine learning and self-driving cars became reality, the tales of a giant bronze creature called Talos, an artificial woman named Pandora, and their creator god, Hephaestus, filled the imaginations of people in ancient Greece.

The story of Talos, first mentioned around 700 BC by Hesiod,[1] offers one of the earliest conceptions of a robot, Adrienne Mayor[2] has suggested.

> The myth describes Talos as a giant bronze man built by Hephaestus, the Greek god of invention and blacksmithing. Talos was commissioned by Zeus, the king of Greek gods, to protect the island of Crete from invaders. He marched around the island three times every day and hurled boulders at approaching enemy ships.
>
> [...]
>
> Although much later versions of the story portray Pandora as an innocent woman who unknowingly opened a box of evil, Mayor said Hesiod's original described Pandora as an artificial, evil woman built by Hephaestus and sent to Earth on the orders of Zeus to punish humans for discovering fire.
>
> [...]
>
> In addition to creating Talos and Pandora, mythical Hephaestus made other self-moving objects, including a set of automated servants, who looked like women but were made of gold, Mayor said. According to Homer's recounting of the myth, Hephaestus gave these artificial women the gods' knowledge. Mayor argues that they could be considered an ancient mythical version of AI.[3]

DOI: 10.4324/9781003175063-3

First Beginnings and Winters

The field of AI research was founded at a workshop held on the campus of Dartmouth College, in Hanover, New Hampshire, where the term 'artificial intelligence' was coined during the summer of 1956, before even the author of this book was born.

But achieving progress in this new field was challenging; interest in the field dropped off from 1974 to 1980 (which became known as the first 'AI Winter') but the field later revived in the 1980s when the British government started funding it again in part to compete with efforts by the Japanese.

The field experienced a second 'AI Winter' from 1987 to 1993, mostly due to reduced government funding.

But research slowly resumed and in 1997, IBM's Deep Blue[4] became the first computer to beat a chess grand master when it defeated Garry Kasparov. And in 2011, the IBM system 'Watson'[5] won the quiz show *Jeopardy!*[6] by beating the reigning champions.

High Points from Fantasy to Reality

Here are some 'high points' in the AI journey, or rise of the machines, that clearly show that the 'AI Winters' of the past are exactly that, history, and not part of the present or future:

> 1637 – Long before robots were even a feature of science fiction, scientist and philosopher Rene Descartes[7] pondered the possibility that machines would one day think and make decisions. He identified a division between machines which might one day learn about performing one specific task, and those which might be able to adapt to any job. Today, these two fields are known as narrow and general AI.
>
> 1726 – Jonathan Swift[8] published *Gulliver's Travels*, which includes a description of the 'Engine', which is possibly the earliest known reference to a device in any way resembling a modern computer. The Engine is a device that generates permutations of word sets. It is found at the Academy of Projectors in Lagado, '...everyone knew how laborious the usual method is of attaining to arts and sciences; whereas, by his contrivance, the most ignorant person, at a reasonable charge, and with a little bodily labour, might write books in philosophy, poetry, politics, laws, mathematics, and theology, without the least assistance from genius or study'.[9]
>
> 1921 – Czech writer Karel Čapek[10] introduced the word 'robot' in his play 'Rossum's Universal Robots'; the word 'robot' comes from the word 'robota', meaning 'work'.

1956 – The Dartmouth Conference took place, where John McCarthy[11] coined the term 'artificial intelligence'.

1966 – ELIZA, developed at MIT[12] by Joseph Weizenbaum,[13] was the world's first chatbot – and a direct precursor to the likes of Alexa and Siri as it was the first to vocalise communication.

1980 – Digital Equipment Corporation's XCON expert learning system was credited with generating annual savings for the company of $40 million. This is significant because until this point AI systems were generally regarded as impressive technological feats with limited real-world usefulness.

1988 – A statistical approach. IBM[14] researchers published *A Statistical Approach to Language Translation*, introducing principles of probability into the until-then rule-driven field of machine learning. It tackled the challenge of automated translation between human languages – French and English.

1991 – The birth of the Internet. CERN researcher Tim Berners-Lee put the world's first website online and published the workings of the hypertext transfer protocol (HTTP); it does not get much 'bigger' or 'impactful' than that.

1997 – Deep Blue defeated world chess champion Garry Kasparov.

2005 – The DARPA Grand Challenge. This was the second year that DARPA held its Grand Challenge – a race for autonomous vehicles across over 100 kilometres of off-road terrain in the Mojave Desert. In 2004, none of the entrants managed to complete the course. The following year, five vehicles successfully completed the course, with the team from Stanford University taking the prize for the fastest time.

2011 – IBM Watson's *Jeopardy!* win.

2012 – The true power of deep learning was unveiled to the world. Researchers at Stanford and Google published a paper, 'Building High-Level Features Using Large Scale Unsupervised Learning', building on previous research into multilayer neural nets known as deep neural networks. Specifically, they singled out the fact that their system had become highly competent at recognising pictures of cats.

2014 – The 'Turing' test[15] was (arguably) achieved for the very first time by computer programme 'Eugene Goostman',[16] although many suggest that since it only convinced a third of the 'judging' humans, it was a mute success, and since it profiled as a 13-year-old boy it had a default level of lack of knowledge that could be explained to the 'humans' when it could not answer questions.

2015 – Machines could now 'see' better than humans. Researchers studying the annual ImageNet challenge (where algorithms compete to show their proficiency in recognising and describing a library of images) declared that machines are now outperforming humans.

2016 – Gameplay has long been a chosen method for demonstrating the abilities of thinking machines, and AlphaGo,[17] created by DeepMind, defeated world *Go*[18] champion Lee Sedol over five matches. Although *Go* moves can be described mathematically, the sheer number of the variations of the game that can be played (there are over 100,000 possible opening moves in *Go*, compared to 400 in chess) make the brute force approach impractical. AlphaGo used neural networks to study the game and learn as it played.

2018 – Self-driving cars hit the roads.

2020 to present – Many amazing points of progression, too many to note here (I do encourage you to do some personal research on this), but one that is well placed in this current (as I write this book) pandemic is the achievement of COVID-19 detection in lungs by AI. Scientists at the University of Central Florida conducted a study to use AI in the detection of COVID-19 in the lungs and the outcome was as accurate as a specialist medical doctor. They trained AI algorithms to identify COVID-19 pneumonia with 90 percent accuracy via computer tomography (CT) scans. It has identified 84 percent positive and 93 percent negative cases to date.

The rise of the machines has to be acknowledged as something pretty amazing and the acceleration in development, and successes, seems to be exponential.

Time to move on to explore how this rise of AI will change project management forever.

Notes

1 Hesiod was an ancient Greek poet generally thought to have been active between 750 and 650 BC, around the same time as Homer.
2 Adrienne Mayor is a historian of ancient science and a classical folklorist. Mayor specialises in ancient history and the study of 'folk science', or how pre-scientific cultures interpreted data about the natural world, and how these interpretations form the basis of many ancient myths, folklore, and popular beliefs.
3 Alex Shashkevich, 'Stanford researcher examines earliest concepts of artificial intelligence, robots in ancient myths'. *Stanford News*, 28 February 2019. https://news.stanford.edu/2019/02/28/ancient-myths-reveal-early-fantasies-artificial-life/

4 Deep Blue was a chess-playing computer developed by IBM. It was the first computer to win both a chess game and a chess match against a reigning world champion under regular time controls.
5 Watson is a question-answering computer system capable of answering questions posed in natural language, developed in IBM's DeepQA project by a research team led by principal investigator David Ferrucci. Watson was named after IBM's founder and first CEO, industrialist Thomas J. Watson.
6 *Jeopardy!* is a classic game show – with a twist. The answers are given first, and the contestants supply the questions.
7 René Descartes was a French-born philosopher, mathematician, and scientist who spent a large portion of his working life in the Dutch Republic.
8 Jonathan Swift was an Anglo-Irish satirist, essayist, political pamphleteer, poet, and Anglican cleric who became Dean of St Patrick's Cathedral, Dublin.
9 Jonathan Swift, *Gulliver's Travels*, originally titled *Travels into Several Remote Nations of the World, in Four Parts. By Lemuel Gulliver, First a Surgeon, and then a Captain of several Ships*, 1726, amended 1735. Full text at Project Gutenberg. The quotation is an extract from *Part III; A Voyage to Laputa, Balnibarbi, Luggnagg, Glubbdubdrib, and Japan*; Chapter V.
10 Karel Čapek was a Czech writer, playwright, and critic. He has become best known for his science fiction, including his novel *War with the Newts* and play *R.U.R.*, which introduced the word 'robot'.
11 John McCarthy was an American computer scientist and cognitive scientist. McCarthy was one of the founders of the discipline of artificial intelligence.
12 MIT, the Massachusetts Institute of Technology, is a private land-grant research university in Cambridge, Massachusetts.
13 Joseph Weizenbaum was a German-American computer scientist and a professor at MIT. The Weizenbaum Award is named after him. He is considered one of the fathers of modern AI.
14 IBM, the International Business Machines Corporation, is an American multinational technology company headquartered in Armonk, New York, with operations in over 170 countries.
15 The Turing test, originally called the imitation game by Alan Turing in 1950, is a test of a machine's ability to exhibit intelligent behaviour equivalent to, or indistinguishable from, that of a human.
16 Eugene Goostman is a chatbot that some regard as having passed the Turing test, a test of a computer's ability to communicate indistinguishably from a human.
17 AlphaGo is a computer programme that plays the board game *Go*. It was developed by DeepMind Technologies, which was later acquired by Google. Subsequent versions of AlphaGo became increasingly powerful, including a version that competed under the name Master.
18 *Go* is an abstract strategy board game for two players in which the aim is to surround more territory than the opponent. The game was invented in China more than 2,500 years ago and is believed to be the oldest board game continuously played to the present day.

Thoughts from the Real World:

'I think the idea of using AI for Project Management is exciting. The possibilities of having "intelligence" help us with providing information that is non-emotion based'.

'As a PM I am communicating with people all the time. Sometimes I need just to listen to them or give advice, award someone or downgrade others... or just bring chocolate to someone who is desperate. No AI could do that when it comes to people'.

Chapter 4

Categories of AI

Is AI and project management a valuable partnership?

Perhaps to answer, or at least begin to answer, that question, we all need a little more insight and understanding of what makes up AI.

There are four main categories of AI: project management process automation, project assistant style chatbots, project intelligence through machine learning, and the future state of the autonomous project manager.

Process Automation

Also known as business process automation, process automation is the ability to coordinate and integrate tools, people, and processes through a defined workflow.

Process automation aims to reduce human errors, enable faster responses to issues and decision making, and to allow a more efficient allocation of resources for greater overall efficiency. It also does this across a full portfolio landscape, taking into account the maximum amount of data available for greater insight and a more balanced output.

Examples might be enabling auto-scheduling by means of programmed logic and rules, automatically tracking the progress and status of tasks performed by project team members and alerting a (human) project manager for intervention only by exception, using exception-based management for optimum performance.

Chatbots

A chatbot is a software application used to conduct an online chat conversation via text or text-to-speech, in lieu of providing direct contact with a live human agent. It can automate conversations and interact with people through messaging platforms.

DOI: 10.4324/9781003175063-4

At the heart of chatbot technology lies natural language processing or NLP, the same technology that forms the basis of the voice recognition systems used by virtual assistants such as Google Now, Apple's Siri, and Microsoft's Cortana.

We are all probably most aware of chatbots through interaction with such technology, and also with the delight of 'chatbotting' our way through a customer support system when something has gone wrong with a service or product.

In project management, chatbots can act as project assistants interacting with the (human) project manager in human–computer interaction, based on speech or text recognition. Chatbots will be able to take over menial tasks such as organising meetings, progress management tracking, and team reminders plus more.

Machine Learning

Machine learning enables predictive analytics and can provide advice to the (human) project manager on how to guide the project given certain parameters or how to respond to issues and risks, always with the driving purpose of reaching the best possible outcome for the project.

There are four strands of learning for machine learning:

- Supervised learning: Data is labelled and the algorithm is trained to correlate each data set with the labelled result – for example: diagnosing x-ray results.
- Unsupervised learning: Data is not labelled but with sufficient number of indicating guides the algorithm will be able to classify data correctly –for example: in genetics, clustering DNA patterns to analyse evolutionary biology.
- Reinforcement learning: The algorithm learns through trial and error to make predictions – for example: AI agents are used by DeepMind[1] to cool Google Data Centers, taking snapshots of data every five minutes and feeding this to deep neural networks to predict how different combinations will affect future energy consumptions.
- Rules-based learning: This involves capturing a set of rules that represent all of the knowledge about the data set – for example: an expert system might help a doctor choose the correct diagnosis based on a cluster of symptoms.

The Autonomous Project Manager

Think about those self-driving cars, autonomous vehicles. An autonomous project manager system would only need limited input from a human (presumably an experienced project manager); it would be mostly self-sufficient due to the application of a range of AI technologies, a learning programme suite, and real-time data inputs contrasted against historical project data.

Besides technical project management processes, which are what the previous three AI categories are primarily focused on, an autonomous project management system will additionally need to comprehensively consider and master the project environment and related stakeholders (the people), with all of the associated dynamics and inconsistencies (typically). This is a significantly complicated landscape of static 'facts' and a constantly changing environment of 'opinion', 'conflicting biases', and 'personal priorities', as every project manager knows only too well.

Marc Lahmann of PwC[2] said: 'These AI systems would therefore have to be able to apply sentimental analysis algorithms to crawl through customer communications and understand stakeholder satisfaction and commitment at any given point in time'.

There are currently no real-life examples of fully autonomous project management.

Is It AI?

How can you tell if it's true AI – (strong) artificial intelligence?

Well, the following tests to confirm human-level AGI have been considered:

- The Turing Test (Turing[3])
  - A machine and a human both converse, sight unseen, with a second human, who must evaluate which of the two is the machine, which passes the test if it can fool the evaluator a significant fraction of the time. Note: Turing does not prescribe what should qualify as intelligence, only that knowing that it is a machine should disqualify it.
- The Coffee Test (Wozniak[4])
  - A machine is required to enter an average American home and figure out how to make coffee: find the coffee machine, find the coffee, add water, find a mug, and brew the coffee by pushing the proper buttons.[5]
- The Robot College Student Test (Goertzel[6])
  - A machine enrols in a university, taking and passing the same classes that humans would, and obtaining a degree.
- The Employment Test (Nilsson[7])
  - A machine works an economically important job, performing at least as well as humans in the same job.

Eugene, a computer designed at England's University of Reading, was the first AI to pass the Turing test, in 2014. Eugene was a Russian-designed AI that won because it was designed to sound like an adolescent boy. His creator's reasoning was that '[Eugene] can claim that he knows anything, but his age also makes it perfectly reasonable that he doesn't know everything'.[8]

Steve Wozniak has achieved the Turing test a number of times with Mitsuku, an animated chatbot that calls itself 'an artificial life form living on the net'. It fooled some humans into thinking it was also human and won the Loebner Prize's[9] Turing test competition for the third time since 2013. Steve Wozniack commented 'I believe that the Turing test goal of trying to achieve a human level of intelligence was a noble goal in its day, but computers are capable of doing so much more than a human, especially with memory and information retrieval'.[10]

How Much Data?

A common question regarding AI is 'how much data do we need to make it "work"?', perhaps with a follow-on question about how good the quality of that data needs to be.

The answer is 'it depends' (isn't that always the answer?).

Paul Boudreau, in his book, *Applying Artificial Intelligence to Project Management*, provides a potential answer, referencing Stephen Thomas's lecture on 'AI and Analytics in Business':

> For a proper medical diagnosis, a lot of historical data is needed. For a self-driving care, a lot of live streaming data is required. For business models, somewhat less data is required, and it has been suggested that as few as thirty sets of data might be enough for an AI algorithm.[11]

That said, he also notes: 'In fact, data scientists and machine learning specialists are unable to determine the exact amount of data required.'

Markus Feigelbinder suggested:

> The amount of data needed to train a system sufficiently depends on different factors:
>
> - The complexity of the system: The more parameters in the project, the more data required to train the machine. A system that deals with a specific object will require much less training data than one that accepts input and makes choices.
> - The training method used: Different training methods have different learning curves and data requirements. For example,

systems trained using structured learning methods need less training data than those that rely on deep learning models.
- Diversity of input data: If many types of input are expected, you will need more training data to coach the system to respond to each input type effectively.
- Error tolerance: The purpose of your AI or machine learning project will dictate its tolerance for errors. For example, mistakes can be tolerated in customer service systems but not in patience support machines. Machines with low error tolerance require more data to train.[12]

He concludes by stating: 'There's no need to have a million unnecessary data points if just 100 detailed and clean data points can serve the intended purpose'.

There is another perspective of course, the quality of the data itself. Stéphane de Vroey, a professional in project management culture deployment, noted in my survey:

> As far as I know AI is based on learning patterns; I see three main issues there, and I strongly believe that people selling AI for project management are just deliberately ignoring those...
>
> We do not document our project with enough details to allow any automated learning patterns; historical data remains an issue. Humans tend to hide project problems and failure. See how many projects remain 'Amber' while they are absolute Red Flag ones.
>
> By definition, a project is "Unique Endeavour"; you could never demonstrate that AI has done better than a real project manager (in honesty: the opposite is also true).

Interesting thoughts for sure and think about this as well in regard to data, and data volumes:

> The Data Never Sleeps research by cloud technology firm Domo calculates that, every minute of every day, the internet carries 3.1 million gigabytes of traffic globally, including 159 million emails, 473,400 tweets, and 97,222 hours' worth of Netflix content. It is predicated that by 2020 some 1.7 MB of data will be created every second for every person on Earth. An estimated 90% of the world's data was generated in just the last two years, and the rise of smart-sensor equipped devices – connected by the Internet of Things – will generate further exponential growth.[13]

We certainly will not be short of data, that is for certain.

Notes

1. DeepMind Technologies is a British artificial intelligence subsidiary of Alphabet Inc. and research laboratory founded in September 2010.
2. PwC, 'AI will transform project management. Are you ready?' 2018. https://docplayer.net/152761742-Ai-will-transform-project-management-are-you-ready.html
3. While the Turing test has long served as a milestone for AI developers, advances like self-driving cars, speech processing, and image recognition have rendered the test less relevant.
4. Steve Wozniak, American electronics engineer, cofounder, with Steve Jobs, of Apple Computer Company, and designer of the first commercially successful personal computer.
5. Milk and sugar presumably added to taste (or do AI robots only take it straight?), or perhaps that is yet another dimension to this test, interacting with humans to identify their specific needs (think complicated Starbucks orders for example – mine is a Grande Caramel Macchiato extra hot please).
6. Ben Goertzel is the CEO and founder of SingularityNET, a project combining AI and blockchain to democratise access to AI. Goertzel was the Chief Scientist of Hanson Robotics, the company that created Sophia the Robot, who we will meet later in the book.
7. Nils John Nilsson was an American computer scientist. He was one of the founding researchers in the discipline of AI.
8. Ajit Niranjan, 'Supercomputer passes Turing Test by convincing judges it's a 13-year-old Ukrainian boy'. *New Statesman*, 9 June 2014. www.newstatesman.com/sci-tech/2014/06/supercomputer-passes-turing-test-fooling-judges-its-13-year-old-ukrainian-boy
9. The Loebner Prize is an annual competition in AI that awards prizes to the computer programmes considered by the judges to be the most human-like. The format of the competition is that of a standard Turing test.
10. Blaise Zerega, 'The Turing test is tired. It's time for AI to move on'. *Medium*, 20 September 2017.
11. Paul Boudreau, *Applying Artificial Intelligence to Project Management*, 2019. Referencing Stephen Thomas, lecture on 'AI and analytics in business, machine learning and artificial intelligence'. Ottawa, May 2018.
12. Markus Feigelbinder, 'How much data do I really need to start my fancy AI start-up?' LinkedIn, 16 September 2019. www.linkedin.com/pulse/how-much-data-do-i-really-need-start-my-fancy-ai-markus-feigelbinder/
13. APM, 'Projecting the future: A big conversation about the future of the project profession', 2019. www.apm.org.uk/media/37473/ptf_msgd_ch1-v8_digital.pdf

Thoughts from the Real World:

> 'Project Management is all about leading people towards pre-defined goals. AI will not be capable of leading people in any foreseeable future'.

> 'I am intrigued at the potential of AI in project management but welcome any automated process that will help reduce the manual legwork of project personnel to manage, control, monitor, evaluate, and report on portfolio, programme, and project progression'.

Chapter 5

Explainable AI

Peter: In this chapter, Craig Mackay shares his personal and business experience with AI as he and his colleagues at Sharktower[1] explore the world of explainable AI and the practical value to project management.

Machine learning/AI models are very much seen as black box solutions because they are closed, non-intuitive, and difficult for people to understand. This brings key challenges to adoption, such as trustworthiness, reliability, and rationality. The outputs of machine learning models can have significant impact and unintended consequences.

> By far the greatest danger of Artificial Intelligence is that people conclude too early that they understand it.
>
> (Eliezer Yudkowsky[2])

Many will have seen the high-profile 2018 Reuters[3] report into Amazon's early attempt to streamline their recruiting processes with a machine learning model designed to scan CVs[4] and identify the best candidates. However, having been trained on existing practices and historic data, the AI taught itself that male candidates were preferable and amplified the previous biases against women. I will touch on some project management examples of this later.

There are many examples like the above that highlight, when unchecked, that blindly using AI output could have far-reaching consequences for our organisations. To build trust and identify how we can reliably use AI output, we need to robustly test model output and how people consume it.

In this chapter, I will attempt to introduce the hot topic of Explainable AI (XAI) in data science, challenge our expectations in this area, but more importantly I want to highlight the need to make any data output usable for the end user through actionable insights – where science and design converge.

DOI: 10.4324/9781003175063-5

But as a Simon Sinek[5] has taught us, lets 'start with why'.

A Question of Trust and Reliability

> Vision without action is merely a dream. Action without vision just passes the time. Vision with action can change the world.
>
> (Joel A. Barker[6])

I have used the above quote in nearly every project management training course I have run over the last 20 years.

For me it is still the most important principle of project delivery. We have all seen inspirational leaders that stand up in front of our companies and proclaim a vision of new operating models, innovative new products, or enhanced customer experiences; only for it never to materialise because no plan or action was taken to get there. Or worse still, we see large functions of businesses and middle management in perpetual reactive mode, making one change after another, taking constant action but without clear direction or focus.

Happily, businesses have identified this and advances in data technology are enabling many organisations to start embedding a culture of data-driven decision making throughout; however, the demand and pace of change is ever increasing. Every industry is now experiencing the disruption of digitisation and the data revolution, making it easier for challengers to rapidly enter the market and providing consumers with more choice than ever. For incumbent enterprises it presents risk and a potential challenge to their position as market leaders. This means a need for more pivotal actions and enterprise agility.

According to a 2019 KPMG report,[7] 67 percent of global chief executives agree that 'acting with agility' is the new currency of business; if their businesses are too slow in responding to consumer needs, they will quickly become irrelevant.

The biggest barrier to enterprise agility is rarely capital, skills, technology, or innovation; this is proven by the rapid rise of challenger brands with limited resources. Instead, larger organisations are often constrained by their legacy culture, lack of overall insight, and inability to make effective decisions fast. We know data can break down these barriers.

When it comes to meeting consumer needs, businesses can no longer provide out of the box, one-size-fits-all experiences. Businesses need to provide adaptive buying experiences and product options. In addition, they need to include their customers in product development and innovation, which brings true consumer-led insight but also has the benefit of increasing brand loyalty.

Having access to real-time and visualised monitoring of your customer data, their journeys, and continuous feedback of their experience is vital. This data should be utilised daily to direct where resources are focused in response to customer demands and where there is a need to develop product/service offerings.

Finally, businesses do not only need to measure the right thing to do from a consumer perspective but also utilise data-driven insights to monitor how they are continually delivering against this. This ensures they can start, stop, or pivot projects to maximise their innovation investment and outcome realisation through better and faster decision making.

All of this increases the imperative for using data-driven and AI solutions to underpin identification, prioritisation, and measurement of what business change is required and how we deliver against it. This will have huge implications for how we as project leaders operate and make decisions over the next decade.

With so much data being unlocked and so many impacting variables, the reliance on machine learning to accelerate our ability to analyse and make these decisions will become greater, if not critical.

Our use of data and subsequent decision-making processes are subject to huge legal and regulatory oversight. We need to be able to demonstrate rationale, fairness, and equality in our decision making. A simple misplaced digit or incorrect data source can result in millions of additional costs in mega projects. All the time, businesses and individuals are subject to dispute and litigation on the back of mistakes in their decision making (intentional or not).

So, it is only natural as we accelerate our use of AI that trust and 'explainability' will be a major discussion point.

How can we, and should we, trust the 'black box' in machine learning where even the data scientists and developers cannot explain how a specific decision was arrived at by AI?

So, What Is Explainable AI?

It is worth stating at the outset that I am not a data scientist or machine learning engineer; I have been a change manager and project leader for over 20 years. However, I am lucky to have worked with some great data scientists who have given me the benefit of their patience and knowledge. So hopefully I can share a little insight on the subject of AI in project management with the warning that there will be a fair bit of generalisation used here (I apologise to all data scientists in advance!).

Explainable AI (XAI) is a machine learning application that is interpretable enough that it provides humans a degree of qualitative, functional understanding that can allow the user to understand how the input features (data sets) affect a model's output or it can be more detailed in providing the user with an explanation of how a specific decision or output was derived.

Ultimate XAI looks at why a decision was made so that machine learning outputs can be more interpretable for human users and enable them to understand why the system arrived at a specific decision or performed a specific action. XAI helps provide a level of transparency to AI, potentially making it possible to open up the black box and make the decision-making process easily comprehensible to humans.

It is important to acknowledge that there many limitations of explainability; the type of learning algorithms used to generate a model is a key factor and the type of input data used can be equally important. While we might be able to interpret how a model might get to a decision, that alone may not be sufficient in providing a useful explanation of a decision. Interpretability may be limited to a graphical representation of the main features that influenced a decision. This can be especially useful but viewing features by importance can overlook the interactions and correlation between features that a model may have derived in coming to a decision.

There are many other factors such as the problem domain itself, data processing applied, and types of model predictions used that will make explainability easier or harder. Interpretability is a characteristic of a model that is generally considered to come at a cost.

As a rule of thumb, the more complex the model, the more accurate it is, but the less interpretable it is.

Some key considerations:

- Feature importance: Most model analysis focuses on finding the important features, but they can largely ignore the interactions between features (data sets).
- Problem domain: Each business problem or process will have a complex network of actors and effects. Each real-world problem has its own domain nuances and defining data sets. If model analysis has less of it, the outcome of the explanation will be blurred or too generalised.
- Data pre-processing: To what extent data has already been processed (e.g. dimensionality reduction, word vectorisation, etc.) can obscure the original human meaning and makes the data somewhat less informative.
- Correlated input features: During feature analysis and the selection process, most of the correlations are either dropped to improve accuracy or swamped by other powerful features with more predictive powers. This can hide latent correlation factors from the model and could lead to incorrect explanation.

- Type of prediction: Straightforward binary or ordinal classification and linear regression models are easier to explain as they have natural decision direction. However, models like multi-class classification which do not have inherent order are more difficult to explain.

XAI is a relatively new but rapidly advancing field and there are many techniques that can be called upon by data scientists to help understand the 'black box'. It will often require a blended approach whether we are looking for deep learning explanation to learn about explainable features, using interpretable models to learn more about structured causal models, or utilising model induction methods that run experiments to best *infer* explainability from any model as black box.

However, before you go down a rabbit hole of complexity there is a big BUT coming...

Don't Expect to Comprehend the Unexplainable

Let us assume we are mainly speaking about machine learning. At a basic level, AI can be spilt into general artificial intelligence (GAI), which is intended to learn and think for itself, and narrow artificial intelligence (ANI). ANI is a category of technologies that relies on algorithms and programmatic response to simulate intelligence to support a specific task. Machine learning is a specific type of ANI. Most of the AI applications we are talking about in project management today will be machine learning.

To simplify this even further (again sorry to the data scientists that will inevitably shout at me), machine learning is just labelling based on learning from examples or training data. What is special is not needing user (or programmer) instructions in how to do this labelling, pattern finding, or making predictions.

Image identification is the most commonly used example. It takes us humans the tiniest fraction of a second to scan an image, process it, and identify that it contains, say, a dog; not just a dog but its colour, its breed, and at the same time we can identify all the objects in the background. Now you cannot explain how you processed all that data and how you inherently knew it was a dog; you just do. Our brain computers have thousands of years of evolution and were supplied from a young age with training data. You were shown plenty of example images of dogs and example images of other animals that were not dogs; so hopefully you do not confuse a dog with a lion!

So, if you cannot explain how you identified the dog, it would be extremely difficult for you to instruct a computer to do it with traditional programming language. With AI we can simply supply machine learning models with lots of examples and non-examples and then ask the right questions. The beauty of AI is we do not need to worry about building instructions to solve problems ourselves: the algorithms do that.

We can programme tasks that have a fair degree of logic, workflow, or decision tree determination to them. We can even utilise robotic process automation (RPA[8]) to watch us and automate the capture of these logic tasks and then take over the processing. However, some tasks are so complicated that we cannot automate them by giving explicit instructions.

If the advantage of AI is to help us automate what is unexplainable and near impossible to instruct, how can we expect to then unravel it or even comprehend the complexity of these instructions if we could? 'Arrgghh!', I can hear you all scream at this point.

Before being overwhelmed by the complexity, and expecting data scientists to perform miracles, we need to be pragmatic and consider how the AI output is being used. Of course, if you are expecting the machine to provide a robust decision that will be used without intervention for business- or people-critical decisions, then please spend a lot of time ensuring models are explainable and trustworthy. If you are only looking for faster analysis of large data sets to provide an element of prediction and augmented intelligence that will still have human intervention to investigate, then it does not need to be quite so robust.

For the most part, our use of machine learning will not require this degree of interpretability and explainability. Of course, in fields of advanced analytics with machine learning or AI research this will be important, but for most of us, more important than explainability is testing.

Testing is key to building trust in the output of machine learning models. Testing that the models are performing to the required degree of accuracy or results – ultimately do the models outperform humans in the required tasks or decisions? Testing for overfitting, a common problem in data science where a model can predict outcomes with great accuracy based on the original training data set but performs much worse on new previously unseen data sets. Testing for bias in the data used to train models (as in the Amazon recruitment example), measuring for statistical parity that different groups (of gender, race, age, sexuality etc.) have equal probability of achieving a favourable outcome. This is a huge subject and another book in its own right.

Ultimately, this is a job for your data scientists or machine learning engineers when selecting and testing which models to apply to which problems. However, as change, project, or business leaders that will use or implement machine learning solutions, we should be cognisant of the importance of testing and of the challenges of explainability when seeking to gain adoption and trust in the use of AI.

Example: Picking on People from Fife: My First Failure with AI

For context, Fife is a region in Scotland that is favourable for commuters working in the capital Edinburgh, and in the past its road access used to be serviced by only the Forth Road Bridge (or an awfully long re-routing) that was often subject to closures for accidents, repairs, and adverse weather.

In a previous role, I had experimented with machine learning for predicting project performance, criticality, and the automation of resource allocation. The model was trying to ensure for mission-critical projects, where any slippage was not an option, that we could quickly and unemotionally allocate the best colleagues to support it. Key features that we had to train the model on that related to people were of course skills, experience, performance, plus all their personal attributes such as location.

The model actually worked quite well; it was able to provide suggested high-performing colleagues with the right skills that could be re-allocated based on current work being lower priority. It could potentially save hours of horse-trading between resource managers or project managers not wanting to give up currently allocated team members to other projects.

However, after running the experiment several times, it was by chance that a couple of the team involved noticed they never got selected for critical projects. Even though they were deemed to be the best qualified. They were both from Fife. This is where statistical parity testing may have come in useful to help mitigate this.

At the time, our techniques were a bit more rudimentary but by running experiments of excluding different features, we were able to determine that one of the biggest factors impacting the allocation was meeting timeliness. One of our data sets was on project meeting performance, including rescheduling rates and attendance rates.

What the data showed was people from the Fife region were more likely to reschedule project meetings and had lower attendance rates. They still performed as high as others, worked the same number of hours, and had the requisite skills. In fact, the data set on meeting performance was the one with the biggest variance of all data sets.

Our conclusion was that because of the higher propensity of commuting issues due to the bridge closures, our colleagues from Fife had the biggest disparity in meeting performance; because all other data sets did not have much differentiation, this was discounting them nearly every time from selection on key projects. This would have hugely disadvantaged those colleagues living in Fife.

> Another conclusion was that how we had built and were using the model meant that level of experience had to be a primary factor. This was rather too simplistic and would have resulted in only experienced people getting opportunities for more experience; it would amplify current issues with diversity on projects and would impact knowledge building etc.
>
> Luckily, it was only an experiment, and it taught me early how quickly we can create unintended consequences from what seems quite simple and logical data. Interestingly, as humans we picked up the correlation in this and potential unintended consequences quickly; the model we used and training data we gave it could never have been expected to. This reinforced the importance of testing model performance and working to remove any bias in training data.

We Are Only Human After All

Rag 'n' Bone Man[9] sang in his 2016 hit 'Human' that 'Cos I'm only human after all, I'm only human after all, don't put your blame on me, don't put the blame on me'.

Every time you ask a colleague a question, do you require a neuroscientist be present to attempt to explain how they came to an answer? Of course not, if only because it would make project steering meetings even more inefficient!

Humans are a complex mess of chemical and electrical processes firing off neurological signals from cell to cell to process huge amounts of input data and recall stored memories. We are prone to huge imbalances in our chemical and energy make-up that can affect our decision making and ability to recall accurate memories. We are full of unconscious bias that has been programmed into our memory (training data) from our social surroundings from birth.

> Two things are infinite: the universe and human stupidity; and I'm not sure about the universe.
>
> (Albert Einstein[10])

As humans we are not completely stupid and do not simply believe anything we are told. We are analytical and get to decide how we use information from others and ourselves to make *informed* choices. We are also particularly good at backing our choices by fitting rationale to the inputs and outputs. However, our brains provide us with a psychological safety net by fabricating these stories of reasoning to help us trust our decision-making ability. Without this, the complexity and anxiety in processing complex information would probably stop us making any decisions ever.

Even when our decisions go wrong, we have a helpful human trait of retrospection and hindsight so that we do not blame ourselves too much, which creates yet more psychological safety to try and protect us from the worst of depression. The behavioural psychology is fascinating and something that mentalists[11] and illusionists make great entertainment out of by demonstrating how fallible our brain is.

My point is, if we need explicit explainability when trusting decision making, then we should all stop now and close down our businesses, because none of us can truly explain how we make decisions today. Even the most data-driven of us.

So, let us give AI a bit of a break here. Let the machine learning algorithms do what we cannot explain ourselves and without expectation that we can fully understand, but of course rigorously test for performance, overfitting, and bias. Let us be honest though: it is not hard to get models to perform better than humans.

Our focus could be better spent on making sure that any output we derive from machine learning models is actionable, drives positive behaviours, and enhances probability of successful decisions.

Augmented Actionable Insight

In my opinion, actionability is as, if not more, important than explainability. Are project managers or stakeholders using the insights or suggested actions presented to them in a positive way that have beneficial impact?

One of the areas that was overlooked for decades in most of areas of management information reporting, and in particular portfolio and project management, is information overload and the need for effective data storytelling. The project management profession has made an industry out of reporting and presenting our stakeholders with endless slide decks of information. Often retrospective, subjective, and untimely.

Filtering the Noise

Projects are complex systems of multiple influencing factors; even the smallest of projects has an endless network of cause-and-effect impacts. Determining cause and filtering the noise from multiple attributing factors is difficult.

Not only are projects complex to model, but typically they have poor historical data and factors that are hard to understand (i.e. behavioural aspects of various actors). Any historical data is heavily biased, subjective, and unreliable as more often than not it did not reflect real delivery detail or accurate completion rates.

Figure 5.1 Filtering the noise

Unfortunately, in project management most of our reporting is focused on what happened in the past and that suffers from significant lag (i.e. the typical two-week cycles to gather data and prepare governance reports). When issues surface in project management, projects are reporting the dreaded 'red' status: this is often well after the root cause and there are multiple impacts causing issues. This is a typical signal and noise issue. Project controls and governance today is mainly focused on the noise, the symptoms, and aftereffects. In the main, it misses the early signals that can predict problems before they occur. I highly recommend reading *The Signal and The Noise* by Nate Silver,[12] a fascinating book on probability and statistics, and how to identify true signals in data from all the noisy irrelevant or misleading data.

Combining Science and Design

For any data output to be useful, it must be understandable, timely (near real time), actionable, and ultimately consumable by the end user. This basic principle holds true whether it is for simple MI reporting, designing systems alerts, or implementing AI.

We humans really struggle with overload and need help filtering the signals to give us focus. If information is presented in a way that negatively interrupts us or is too difficult to consume in the moment, we will often just discount it and move on without action. This is where AI can really aid us but where we will also need strong design principles such as UX/UI and behavioural economics.

With the applications of machine learning models to predict project performance, there are a vast number of estimating, performance, and risk factors that we can predict and could play back to project managers.

However, we need to be cognisant of overload on project managers and consider anything that requires a high degree of interpretation by the end user.

Recommendation models are an area that can help determine what we show and to whom, based on their persona, relevancy, importance, and relational networks (both people and work breakdown). User design is equally important to ensure the information is presented at the right time and in a way that the user can understand. Plus, it is vital that we can measure how people act on insights presented to them, i.e. do they take positive action and does it have beneficial impact on project performance?

Example: Making Project Prediction Models Actionable

This example looks at evolution on a project slippage model we developed. At a high level it is a combination of sensitivity analysis determining risk weighting, flow graph modelling showing network effect, and a TensorFlow[13] computational graph for modelling the forward and backward pass of time effect, with time to complete gamma distribution modelling and simulations of probability of completion.

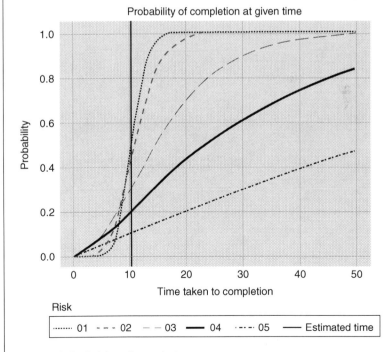

Figure 5.2 Probability of completion

Make sense?

Probably not to most of us (and definitely not to data scientists either as I have oversimplified and skipped bits). It does not really matter as it is not the model I want to discuss or the explainability of the model; but the output of it and how we made that understandable and actionable for project teams. The first step was to try to visualise it.

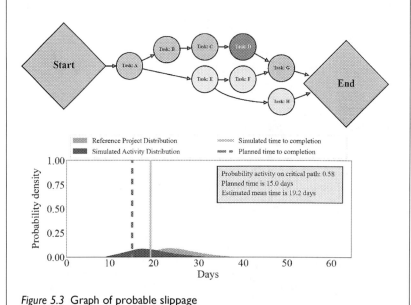

Figure 5.3 Graph of probable slippage

Make sense yet?

Probably not but perhaps with some training it would. The above prototype is showing a graph of probable slippage in days over simulated distributions. It is also a visualisation of the network effect of project activities and which has the greatest influence on slippage, similar to critical path.

There is a fair bit of information represented in that early prototype and it takes a bit of training and interpretation, so it is not especially useful to project managers. However, with some design input we can make the project slippage much easier to convey as shown in Figure 5.4.

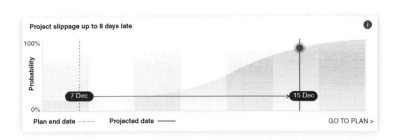

Figure 5.4 Project slippage

Hopefully, this is easier to interpret by anyone; in this example the project is predicted to be up to two weeks late in delivering.

As a project manager what would you do with this output?

Not much is the answer, and you would probably resent the bad news without any explanation. We needed to help project managers understand where they should best focus efforts to help reduce this probable slippage.

The next evolution of the model output was to try and clearly articulate the projected slippage to the project manager but more importantly to easily show them the top activities that were having the greatest impact on this estimate.

Giving them focus without overwhelming them with information, with all activities at risk and the ability to drill down and take action on the priority areas.

Data visualisation, and storytelling, combined with user interface and user experience design, are all key components in making the outputs from AI understandable, actionable, and ultimately trusted.

Our ultimate goal with machine learning should be to automate data insights on project delivery, help project teams spot problems early, and identify where best to focus project management efforts to continually reduce the uncertainty and increase the probability of delivering project outcomes.

Being able to interpret, prioritise, filter, and provide actionable insights at the right time from large amounts of information is absolutely key to enabling people to make effective use of data and take decisions off the back of it.

38   Explainable AI

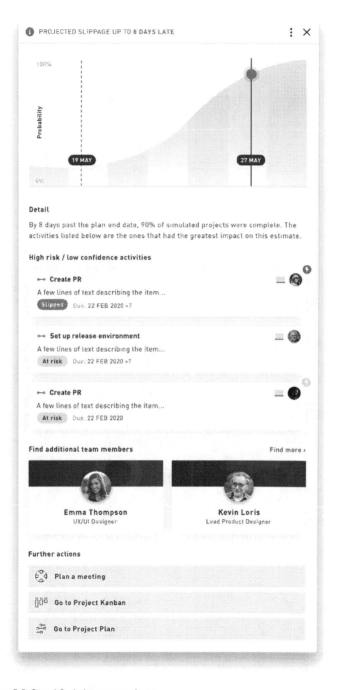

Figure 5.5 Simplified slippage analysis

Being data literate and knowing the art of data storytelling will, I believe, become key skills for project leaders and portfolio management offices as we become more data driven in the future. This is where the broader definition of 'explainability' blends science and design.

Notes

1. Get a clearer view of your projects with Sharktower's AI-driven project management software. From visual planning to automated reporting, you'll see better outcomes across the board. www.sharktower.com
2. Eliezer Yudkowsky is an American AI researcher and writer best known for popularising the idea of friendly AI. He is a co-founder and research fellow at the Machine Intelligence Research Institute, a private research nonprofit based in Berkeley, California.
3. Jeffrey Dastin, 'Amazon scraps secret AI recruiting tool that showed bias against women'. Reuters, 11 October 2018. www.reuters.com/article/us-amazon-com-jobs-automation-insight-idUSKCN1MK08G
4. CV: Curriculum Vitae or Resume.
5. Simon Oliver Sinek is a British-American author and inspirational speaker. He is the author of five books, including *Start With Why* and *The Infinite Game*.
6. Joel Barker was the first person to popularise the concept of paradigm shifts in the corporate world. He began his work in 1975 after spending a year on fellowship meeting and working with visionary thinkers in both North America and Europe.
7. KPMG, 'Leading in uncertain times', 2019. https://home.kpmg/xx/en/home/campaigns/2019/05/leading-in-uncertain-times.html
8. Robotic process automation is a form of business process automation technology based on metaphorical software robots or on AI/digital workers. It is sometimes referred to as software robotics.
9. Rory Charles Graham (born 1985), better known as Rag'n'Bone Man, is a British singer and songwriter. He is known for his deep baritone voice.
10. Albert Einstein was a German-born theoretical physicist, universally acknowledged to be one of the two greatest physicists of all time, the other being Isaac Newton. Einstein developed the theory of relativity, one of the two pillars of modern physics.
11. Mentalism is a performing art in which its practitioners, known as mentalists, appear to demonstrate highly developed mental or intuitive abilities.
12. *The Signal and the Noise: Why Most Predictions Fail – but Some Don't* (alternatively stylized as *The Signal and the Noise: Why So Many Predictions Fail – but Some Don't*) is a 2012 book by Nate Silver detailing the art of using probability and statistics as applied to real-world circumstances. The book includes case studies from baseball, elections, climate change, the 2008 financial crash, poker, and weather forecasting.
13. TensorFlow is a free and open-source software library for machine learning. It can be used across a range of tasks but has a particular focus on training and inference of deep neural networks. TensorFlow is a symbolic math library based on dataflow and differentiable programming.

Thoughts from the Real World:

'AI will free up project managers from tedious duties and will help them to focus on the most relevant part of PM, working with people'.

'Building relationships and genuine and authentic relationships... will AI be able to top that human skill'?

Chapter 6

People-centric AI

Peter: In this chapter, Bentzy Goldman shares his personal and business experience with AI as he and his team at Perflo[1] drive a new people-centric focus on project management. One that I have been delighted to be part of for the last 18 months.

Don't Be a Hater!

Most people would think there is an obvious dichotomy between AI and people, and it is a matter of who will get the 'job to be done'. Many people believe it's a battle and only one side can win. But what if we both win? People don't spend decades researching and developing technologies to replace themselves.

The fear of jobs being replaced, the potential clash between humans and robots, the redundancy, actual or intellectual, all amounts to a classic sci-fi based, doom-laden futuristic nightmare – as in *Metropolis*[2] or more recently *The Terminator*.[3] However, much that is possible (in the coming months and years) with all the technological replacement of that which is the repetitive and mundane part of human collaboration will allow more time to build and develop personal relationships, and this is where the future lies, I believe.

An analogy I tend to overuse is the example of autonomous vehicles. Motorists aren't (or at least I hope they're not) complaining that this advancement has taken away their daily activity of driving and is 'replacing' them. Most can appreciate that what this development now allows them to do is much more powerful than simply steering a wheel. For those lucky enough to own an electric vehicle, traffic is merely an opportunity to work; road trips are opportunities to dedicate more of ourselves to our friends and family and whip out a game of cards. Yes, I will still enjoy a spin in a sports car on the weekend but during the week it has essentially 'freed us of the mundane' and transformed driving into

DOI: 10.4324/9781003175063-6

a much more productive activity, ultimately allowing us to be more efficient and focus on the things we care about.

The way I think of using AI in project management is less about *replacing* our jobs, and more about helping us to be more *efficient* in our jobs, giving us the wonderful opportunity to spend this newfound time in a much more meaningful and purposeful manner.

AI Isn't AI, and You Don't Always Need It Anyway

I'm sorry to now have to dampen the mood, but true AI is a long time away, or so the experts tell me.

True AI doesn't even exist, so naturally I'm always a bit weary and wary of the term being thrown around, especially by startups claiming to use AI in innovative ways, while in essence there is a junior data scientist calculating some type of analytics in a basement in California.

I have come to substitute the acronym for a more tangible description – 'automated intelligence' or 'augmented intelligence' when appropriate.

Some of the top AI researchers in the world estimate there's a 50 percent chance that true AI (sometimes referred to as AGI or 'artificial general intelligence') will only be developed by 2099 (others say 2060). Forgive me for being cynical, but an algorithm created by humans with a certain set of rules and variables is not artificial. The closest we have come are subsets of machine learning, like deep learning as well as a new breakthrough called GPT-3. But regardless, the level of current 'artificial' intelligence does not exceed that of a small child. (as of February 2021).

Deep learning exposes what we know to be true – the superseding intelligence of computers over humans. So as not to offend the humans reading this, or your 'AI-based' text-to-speech reader, I should probably clarify what I mean by 'intelligence'.

In our case, intelligence stems from the mind, the human mind which, although incredibly powerful and being part of the most advanced in the animal species, still has its limitations.

The limitations I refer to are less about storage space and more about speed. You can have unlimited storage space but without a certain level of computational power, you have a lot of unrelated items in different sections without the smart functionality of an Amazon warehouse facility robots shifting them around autonomously to where they need to be. Everything stored needs to be manually moved in and out and placed in the right box, on the right conveyor belt, and that takes a huge amount of time if you want to get a parcel to a customer in under two hours.

So, if we think of the human brain, the possibility of what something like deep learning can do is there, but it would take a human an infinite amount of time to go through even a terabyte of data, identify it and correlate it with millions of other data points, and produce a single piece of insight. As such, the power of a technology like machine learning is incredibly useful for radically shortening the amount of time and resources needed to complete a task or pinpoint a unique piece of insight.

At the core of this is the field of data science. The discipline of data science is simply put as understanding how to get to what we want to know, using data, modelling, and statistics. This is the first step in training a model for the 'machine' to learn from and improve over time.

Actually, I'm wrong, because in actual fact the first step is figuring out what you want to glean from the data and why. The 'why' is a critical and an oftentimes overlooked step in the process. For the cost of data scientists, analysts, developers, and machine learning engineers, you had better have a solid business case for why you need to use machine learning in an attempt to improve efficiency or better understand a root cause. The reason I say it is overlooked is because I see a lot of engineers, teams, and entire organisations committing incredible resources to AI projects and building AI-fuelled products, when in actual fact the same or similar outcome could have been achieved without all that effort and in more cost-effective ways. But like all trends, everyone 'wants in'.

Without Knowing Where You Want to Go, Using a Ferrari Will Only Get You Nowhere Faster

The reason I have begun this chapter with a somewhat cautious approach is because I have made the mistake myself in our business. Not necessarily the 'why' mistake, but more the 'how' mistake, and getting in on AI. The outcome we wanted was truly clear: we wanted to use technology and data in order to understand what made projects succeed or fail and prioritise leveraging the knowledge of the people behind them (people data) and not simply the traditional project data (when the task is complete) most people used. We knew there was a missing piece to project management because we were not project management professionals ourselves and it was immediately clear to us that people were not emphasised as a priority in traditional project management performance measurement.

The first place you need to look to come to this realisation is the training that project managers go through. It is filled with process-oriented materials, project methodologies, and complex reporting but an extraordinarily small amount of material on 'how to build and run a high-performance team' or 'how to ensure your people are supported and happy throughout your project'. Even in the agile world of team retros, the majority of the talk is either technical or project related and not people related.

Furthermore, we wanted to make sure that project leaders had access to this information (people data) during their projects as opposed to at the end of the project, when it is essentially too late to act on. So, we needed to come up with a way to gather data, analyse it, and feed it to project managers throughout the life cycle of their projects. And of course using AI to do it. The first part – a clear mission statement. The second part – a waste of six months and many dollar bills. There are quite a few places in a project one could gather data from, most obviously your project management or PPM[4] tool. Others include communication tools like email and Slack. And of course, anything else you want to upload into your algorithm, whether it be an Excel document or a plain text file. There are also various ways of analysing said data, including one of the most commonly used – NLP (natural language processing).[5]

I now believe that when it comes to people you can never discount the value of qualitative data. If it is about what people feel and what they think and not necessarily what they write on a public channel, email, or even what they say to a manager in a check-in, anonymous feedback reveals the hidden insights you need to run a high-performing team and successful project. Granted, there are times when anonymity isn't helpful; for instance, if you want to detect a specific issue related to a task that is owned by one or two people, anonymity won't give you the clarity you need and may also cause passive conflict as it's generally quite easy to tell who said what with only two people giving feedback.

The power of AI comes in when you can leverage the qualitative feedback and turn that into quantitative analytics. Intelligent analytics, not just the 'health score' of a team. Using the craft of data science and machine learning, the output of this data is incredibly powerful for delivering not only 'deep insights' but also actionable recommendations. Imagine all of this happening in the background throughout your project!

Combining project data, people data, and communication data and leveraging the latest research we, at Perflo, are able to develop a powerful product that guides project managers throughout their projects on how to best empower their teams and where the risks or areas of attention may be, as well as what are the best actions to take to mitigate those risks. For senior leadership, they now have a new world of data, a new world of value in which they can identify recurring trends, themes, and hotspots where they can prioritise resources to empower their managers and teams by knowing exactly what is affecting project success or failure within their organisation. No more will they rely on one tool or one person for data. I dream of the day when PowerPoint reports become obsolete. Sorry Satya.[6]

Instead of project managers spending a good portion of their time compiling and presenting reports, they are fully automated and delivered to the right people at the right time. Again, saving time and allowing for managers and leaders to look at the data more attentively and holistically in order to make informed decisions going forward. These reports and data could be aggregated from all projects, current and historical, to identify these trends and hotspots previously spoken of. It is not always 'the more data the better', but if you have the right data, clean data, accurate data – AI can uncover things you were never previously aware of; it can allow you to make improvements along the way, impacting efficiency, performance, and overall project success rates across the organisation.

So, to finish off this argument, it's all about the context of the use case and more importantly why it's necessary to use AI in that context. It goes without saying to calculate the cost versus benefits of using AI in your projects. Many times (depending on the size/resources of your organisation) it is cheaper and more efficient to use a software vendor as opposed to in-house if they can serve your needs in this case. For one they generally know what they are doing if they have enough customers and a few proven case studies. Second, they have a lot more data (over time) than you and varied data – which means more accurate results and a refined algorithm. This allows for benchmarks which you can compare yourself against. Having said that, they may not always align with your strategy or solve the particular problem in the context of your industry, organisation, and of course projects.

Here are some questions you might want to ask when thinking about applying AI to your PMO/projects:
Do we need to...

1. Analyse vast data sets at scale?
2. Learn at a much faster pace than humans can?
3. Find things humans cannot?
4. Make our jobs easier?
5. Make data-driven decisions faster?

AI-fuelled Coaching of Leaders and Teams

As we discussed previously, with the use of AI, we now have the opportunity for 'autonomous' training or coaching of both managers and teams. Again, it does not replace training per se and the value in putting together training materials for different roles and topics (although that can also be done autonomously) or replace the human element of coaching. What it does do is make the training materials timelier, in the moment; it makes it more digestible; and probably most importantly – more contextual to what is actually going on in the project or team at that exact moment.

Imagine not having to take a break from your job to attend a three-day tedious and boring training workshop, of which most of the material you will forget within a week or two. As opposed to having an intelligent coaching engine which reacts to the various activities in your project as well as the team's performance and engagement levels, guiding you to make the best decisions in the moment to empower your team. I think it is the only sensible way forward (see 'nudge theory' by Richard Thaler[7]).

Project Matching

This leads me into the next use case for using machine learning in project management: the ability to 'match' people on the projects they would be most passionate about working on.

Notice how I've not mentioned skills or capacity here. These both exist and unfortunately are the common basis for assigning people to projects, but the research says something else that most organisations don't take into account. If you are more passionate about the work you're doing, you will put in more effort to the job at hand, take ownership of the work, and be more determined to produce a higher degree of quality work than if you weren't particularly keen on that project.

Skills Can Be Developed, but Engagement Can't

In addition, research shows that having challenging work to a moderate degree impacts job retention. It is completely logical: if the work becomes second nature to you, it essentially becomes admin and admin is boring so, 'sorry boss but I'm leaving my job to find something more stimulating'. Most people do not like to rot away, plus we already know that higher engagement results in increased task performance, which subsequently influences project performance positively. Now although this would require removing some of the anonymous data, I can, with full confidence, guarantee you that employees will have no problem with it if this means they get to work on the things they care about.[8]

This algorithm can be adapted for manager matching as well, using skills, personality, and previous project performance to assign the best managers for their ideal-suited projects. This could mean that a project which is more technical obviously requires technical skills, but more so than that, the type of people on that team require a certain leadership style. Looking at team dynamics in relation to managerial style is the ideal combination to position the project for success. Using skills and capacity are only two parts of the picture: a more holistic analysis is needed in order to account for all variables that we could gather from previous projects and based on the research again of 'what are the true makings of a high-performance project team?'.

Obviously, the more projects that are run and the more similar the project types delivered in the organisation are, then the more accurate the data. Updated skills data as well as accurate leadership data is crucial to make an accurate prediction. I have seen a lot of companies' skills data be as old as five years from when that person was onboarded in their role. An awful lot can happen in five years as we all know; therefore, it is critical to make sure the data is as recent as possible.

Again, a powerful example of a use case where human calculation and interpretation would either be biased or assumptive is when matching the right people to the right projects. Out of the hundreds of people I spoke to in varied industries (all project-based), most organisations matched people to projects based on capacity, and sometimes not even skills. Mainly the need of the project or stakeholder but not on the need or desire of the person being assigned to a project – a rookie error in employee engagement. To get the best out of people is to ensure they are doing work that is a) exciting to them or b) challenging to them, and of course doing that work within a great team and culture. This blend is the holy grail of engagement and retention. The benefits of this extend beyond an isolated project, but rather it can be felt organisation wide if this practice is adopted and implemented correctly.

Prediction

Arguably the most talked about and intriguing of all areas of AI in project management is the ability to predict project success in real time.

PwC[9] states that predictive project analytics will be the most disruptive innovation in project management in the next ten years. There are also 'sub-predictions' that exist in the area of prediction, such as task completion estimations, timelines, and cost, which can aid project managers in understanding their project's progress more accurately and deliver accurate reporting on performance. Essentially prediction mitigates risk – one of the pillars of traditional project management. The ability to predict task completion doesn't necessarily require AI, but let's say you do use some sort of machine learning for this; over time you train the algorithm to understand when (and hopefully why) certain tasks will be delayed based on other tasks being delayed or key words in communication channels or however you design the system – that's irrelevant – what is relevant is ensuring you are continuously learning from the results and of course the root causes. There is no use having insightful data and not learning from it. This goes back to my point that using vendors as opposed to in-house built products provides more accurate data because they have many other companies' data in their algorithm, which means the results will be more precise, and that is exactly what you want. The last thing you need is inaccurate estimations from the wondrous AI algorithm you've invested in.

Shifting back to the topic of this chapter and our passion – people. Imagine being able to predict when the team is going to be overworked, stressed, and ultimately disengaged – which we believe is an even greater risk than an extended task's timeline. Imagine being able to predict whether silos are developing within your team. Again, including people data in project prediction is something that we believe truly is the next leap in project success and a critical part of project management.

Market Predictions in Project Management

Zooming out but at the same time diving deeper into prediction, some organisations have leveraged market prediction methodologies to predict project success. Now although this can be incredibly insightful, there is a way for companies to incorporate some of the learnings from prediction markets into their predictive strategy.

As you may tell, I am a big advocate for qualitative data, and I believe its value is underused in project management. Combining both the qualitative and quantitative in order to predict project delivery and ultimately project success is by far the most powerful way to have an accurate read on project performance. I would even go a step further and incorporate third party data looking outside your organisation and into industry, markets, economies, and even social trends to assess the potential impact from all these variables.

A perfect example of this is when the coronavirus pandemic hit and many projects were all of a sudden put on hold. While the virus was a surprise to all, some had longer prep time than others and the warning signs were definitely there months in advance. Of course, this is all contextual to your project, organisation, industry etc.; however, the philosophy remains consistent and pertinent. 'Project continuity' isn't something frequently talked about, but as we've realised the importance of having a 'business continuity' strategy, perhaps now PMOs will incorporate these learnings into their projects.

To conclude, take as many variables as possible into account when making predictions and, oh, always trust the wisdom of crowds over the wisdom of one project manager.

Project Success Measurement

One of the things that boggled my mind when I stumbled upon the world of project management was the lack of measurement of project impact and business benefits when it came to assessing project performance.[10]

The reasons why are obvious: it is sort of like how an Amazon delivery driver will drop your package at your house; you get the email 'Your package has been delivered' and their job, in relation to you, is done. It is not their concern whether the package will be of good use to you, or how you will use it and benefit from it in the long term (perhaps not the best example since you ordered it). And that is why it is so difficult to measure something in the future when project reviews happen straight after the project. There is a missing piece, but no PMO or project sponsor wants to give out warranties now do they?

As you can tell, I complain (or 're-think') about a lot of things, and I'm not quite done yet, sorry.

Let us, in all seriousness, talk about the famous triple constraint[11] (budget, time, scope). If you have been paying attention, you know what I'm going to say is the fourth constraint – yes that's right, it's none other than 'people' or 'team'. The ones responsible for delivering the scope, on time and on budget (to quality). There is a fifth constraint I haven't mentioned – impact. Personally, I'd rather have a project delivered late with a huge business impact than a project delivered early, with very little business impact. But hey, that's just me.

A Team Is Only as Great as the Sum of Its Parts

I would also make a point to mention that it is always valuable to include project team members in not just the contribution but also the analysis of project performance data as much as possible. A team is only as great as the sum of its parts and there is unspoken knowledge that exists within the heads of sometimes the most introverted souls. Give them an opportunity to add their value to the process.

Now, you may be thinking; 'what the hell does all this have to do with the title of this book?' Give me a minute here. There is a reason I discussed prediction first and talked about variables. It is important to have a baseline, have an end goal, and understand what success looks like before trying to measure it. That goes for an individual project, a programme, a PMO, and of course an entire organisation. Machine learning can help to measure a number of these factors and produce those hidden gems of insights which are 'naked to the project manager's eye' so to speak.

In terms of the bigger picture, AI can help us to identify trends, patterns, and hotspots which require extra attention. These learnings then should be turned into recommendations for current and future projects. If implemented correctly, they should be able to help project managers course correct when facing an issue, either based on what previous project managers did in similar projects or based on learning materials within the system itself which would be triggered at that very moment the issue occurred.

Chatbots for People/Automate Communication Intelligently

We all know communication is at the core of project management and one of the most critical skills all PMs should master. But what if AI could help not only streamline communication but also do some of it for us? Well of course now I'm going to tell you it can. There is an element of this called ONA[12] (organisational network analysis), which essentially monitors patterns of communication and collaboration networks across an organisation. It is not mainstream yet but as the technology democratises, the ability for PMOs and individual project managers to utilise this technology will be immensely powerful when combined with a communication tool to act on insights. There have been chatbots developed for more efficient scheduling or task management but I'm yet to see a true bot which plugs into all of your tools, understands all of the relevant information, and is essentially a replica of a project manager, but acting as their executive assistant. I reckon we could call it a 'super chatbot', because it is not only reactive, but also proactive. Currently chatbots react to what you tell them, but taking initiative isn't one of their strong suits.

How Do We Use AI? Understanding Root Cause in Project Failure

I think it is pretty evident that I'm a staunch believer in using data to make decisions as opposed to intuition. In fact, one of our core values at Perflo is 'Data speaks louder than words', and we've seen it prove itself time and time again, both in positive and negative circumstances. When we drop the ego and listen to the data, wondrous things can happen. It is not a matter of opinion: McKinsey[13] reports that data-driven organisations are not only 23 times more likely to acquire customers, but they're also six times as likely to retain customers and 19 times more likely to be profitable. That should close the case for being data driven.

As I mentioned at the beginning of the chapter, one of our goals was to help teams find out what causes their projects to succeed or fail, and find out during their projects not after, and of course incorporating the people factor in projects and not just the typical project management metrics.

I believe we are just on the cusp of the possibilities for the application of AI in project management, and the area which excites me most is perhaps also the most untouched. Innovation happens when different ideas merge to solve a unique problem and I believe the more outsiders and creatives that inspect the inner workings of project management, the more they are welcomed in to work with practitioners and leaders, and the better the solutions will be produced. The merging of minds, both technical and creative, is a powerful force, one that inspired the birth of some of the world's most valuable companies today.

The Boring but Important: Data Privacy and Ethics

When dealing with data related to employees it is critical to pay attention to (or is sometimes illegal to) how we use certain data, especially in order to analyse performance. Now, when it comes to project management, I doubt there will CCTV installation and ankle bracelets tracking team members' activity; however, there could be instances where generally if the employees know what data is being used and why, and so long as it is in their best personal interest (and not to spy on them or jeopardise their employment), it generally should pass the test. Don't go on my word alone though; I'm no legal expert. With people data, anonymity solves a lot of this and focusing on teams instead of individuals helps mitigate the risk of personal data use.

There is as much an ethical concern as there is a legal concern, and the opportunity cost of demoralising employees, or worse losing their trust in the company, is sometimes not worth it as engagement and retention start to take a hit. The exposure of what social media giants have used personal data for has given way to a wave of the general public's concern and awareness about the protection of personal data. Essentially what's key here is transparency: if everyone is in the loop, comfortable with the data collection in place, then you are in a good place. Most of all, the benefits need to be relayed to employees and stakeholders alike. Generally, if the benefits are clearly understood and make sense to help improve everyone's work in a positive way, the objections you get will likely be the sour apples you'd expect to object anyway.

The best vendors give employees insights as well and not just management. By giving back value, people are encouraged to put more value back in, whether it is in the form of filling out surveys or simply trying to optimise their own productivity through data. Generally, people like to do well in their jobs and if organisations can help them to do that and not simply hoard performance data, everyone is likely to be better off in the bigger picture.

Conclusion: People-centric AI

Over the years, many new methodologies, processes, and ideas that have promised to increase the success rates of projects or at the very least make them delivered less late.

Despite all these advances, companies still face dismal records of punctual projects that stay on budget. Project managers are stressed, team members are working overtime, and of course stakeholders are not happy.

This all sounds like the deep dark world of project management, doesn't it? The good news is that there is light at the end of the tunnel: the light is using the advances in technology, whichever they may be, and freeing up time to focus on the important things – relationships, strategy, and maintaining the wellbeing and engagement of everyone on your team. And of course, make sure the right people are on the right projects!

Passion Over Skills!

I can never say it enough, so I'll say it again: It does not matter whether your methodology is agile or waterfall or hybrid or anything else you might dream up in the future, if the people on your team are not engaged, are not happy, I can guarantee you they will not be dedicated to your project and it is doomed right from the start. On the flip side, if your team is excited about the project and committed to its success, you will have a much higher likelihood of success in the long run.

To conclude, AI is one of the many tools in your arsenal. It is not the be all and end all, it will not solve all your problems, but it can certainly make your life easier if applied correctly.

As the author of this book writes, a lazy project manager isn't lazy, but rather works smarter instead of harder.

When I was a youngling one of my good friend's grandfather used to say to me: 'Bentzy, why make life difficult when you can make it bloody impossible?'. For years, I never understood what that meant, but after running my first few software projects, I quickly came to understand the depth of a seemingly contradictory piece of advice.

Lastly, it's important to keep in mind that AI technologies are constantly developing and maturing, which means that what we think of as 'AI in project management' today will not be the same as that of tomorrow. Thus, it is critical for technologists and practitioners to not only keep abreast of the latest developments, but to continuously work together to create new solutions and solve old problems. Most practitioners are not technologists and most technologists are not practitioners, which is why solutions are often built that aren't solving a problem truly worth solving. If only they (or should I say 'we') worked alongside each other from the start, precious time and money could have been saved. The future is forever brighter – embrace it, be a part of it, but you already are – after all, you're reading this book.

Notes

1 Perflo | High-Performance Project Teams: www.perflo.co. The first project team performance analytics tool, exposing blind spots and bringing project leaders actionable insights at every step of their projects.
2 *Metropolis* is a 1927 German expressionist science-fiction drama film directed by Fritz Lang. Written by Thea von Harbou in collaboration with Lang, the silent film is regarded as a pioneering science-fiction movie, being amongst the first feature-length movies of that genre. *Metropolis* is now widely regarded as one of the greatest and most influential films ever made.
3 *The Terminator* is a 1984 American science fiction film directed by James Cameron. It stars Arnold Schwarzenegger as the Terminator, a cyborg assassin sent back in time from 2029 to 1984 to kill Sarah Connor, whose son will

one day save mankind from extinction by a hostile artificial intelligence in a post-apocalyptic future.

4 Project portfolio management (PPM) is the centralised management of the processes, methods, and technologies used by project managers and project management offices (PMOs) to analyse and collectively manage current or proposed projects based on numerous key characteristics.

5 Natural language processing is a subfield of linguistics, computer science, and AI concerned with the interactions between computers and human language, in particular how to programme computers to process and analyse large amounts of natural language data.

6 Satya Nadella is the Chief Executive Officer of Microsoft.

7 The first formulation of the term and associated principles was developed in cybernetics by James Wilk before 1995 and described by Brunel University academic D. J. Stewart as 'the art of the nudge' (sometimes referred to as micro nudges).

   In 2008, Richard Thaler and Cass Sunstein's book, *Nudge: Improving Decisions About Health, Wealth, and Happiness*, brought nudge theory to prominence. Thaler and Sunstein defined their concept as:

   'A nudge, as we will use the term, is any aspect of the choice architecture that alters people's behavior in a predictable way without forbidding any options or significantly changing their economic incentives. To count as a mere nudge, the intervention must be easy and cheap to avoid. Nudges are not mandates. Putting fruit at eye level counts as a nudge. Banning junk food does not.'

8 There is a way to do this even with anonymous data, but I won't be sharing our trade secrets publicly, sorry!

9 PricewaterhouseCoopers is a multinational professional services network of firms, operating as partnerships under the PwC brand. Marc Lehmann, 'AI will transform project management. Are you ready?' PwC, 2018. https://docplayer.net/152761742-Ai-will-transform-project-management-are-you-ready.html

10 Well, having been in project management for many, many years, it stills boggles my mind so don't be too shocked – Peter Taylor.

11 PMI: Project Management Institute states 'The Triple Constraint says that cost is a function of scope and time or that cost, time and scope are related so that if one changes, then another must also change in a defined and predictable way'. There is also the Iron Triangle – in the mid-1980s, Dr. Martin Barnes created the Triangle of Objectives.

12 Organizational network analysis (ONA) is a structured way to visualise how communications, information, and decisions flow through an organisation. Organisational networks consist of nodes and ties: the foundation for understanding how information in your organization is flowing, can flow, and should flow.

13 Alec Bokman, Lars Fielder, Jesko Perrey, and Andrew Pickersgill, 'Five facts: How customer analytics boosts corporate performance'. McKinsey Global Institute, 1 July 2014. www.mckinsey.com/business-functions/marketing-and-sales/our-insights/five-facts-how-customer-analytics-boosts-corporate-performance McKinsey Global Institute

Thoughts from the Real World:

> 'All professionals should brace for the impact AI will bring to project management and prepare themselves accordingly before the industry is disrupted and their methodologies become obsolete'.

> 'AI is just yet another smoke screen on project management incompetence'.

Chapter 7

Resistance Is Futile

In the wonderful *Hitchhiker's Guide to the Galaxy* series (a trilogy in five parts) by Douglas Adams, the Vogons'[1] battle-cry, and counter-argument to dissent, is 'resistance is useless!'. In the reality of AI and project management, I feel that a similar declaration is applicable, but with a little less of the mindless following orders mindset behind it.

Don't Be a Vogon

I also feel, strongly, that each project leader needs to understand and openly adopt AI through personal effort in learning about and understanding the subject (hopefully this book will help that in some way; it has certainly helped me, as I researched and spoke to people during the development of 'AI and the Project Manager'), and it helped people to consider how this can and will be applied in their own work, their own projects, their own organisation, and to appreciate and welcome the potential future of AI in project management.

I find it very encouraging that in response to my survey question 'How do you "feel" about the rise of AI in project management?' respondents, for the most part, felt positive about AI in their world.

It is good to know that most project managements seem to not be adopting the Vogon approach of 'resistance is useless!' but are openly embracing the art of the AI possible instead.

A comfortingly small number of people felt scared by the 'rise' of AI in their profession (2 respondents) and a few felt concerned (3 respondents), but the majority were somewhere between intrigued and exciting (59 and 50 respondents, respectively). Quite an overwhelming percentage 'on board' and not 'resisting' AI it seems.

Two people, apparently, had no interest (although it seems enough of an interest to respond to a survey on AI in project management).

A further survey question was 'Do you personally think that AI will change project management?' which was aimed at understanding

DOI: 10.4324/9781003175063-7

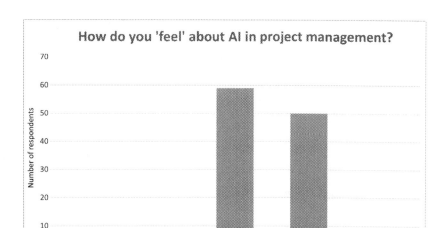

Figure 7.1 How do you 'feel' about AI in project management?

the perceived impact it would have on project managers and project management.

The results are shown in Figure 7.2.

A single respondent felt that nothing would change (perhaps this would be on 'resistor' in the future, or perhaps they were yet to be convinced) and project management would go on as is right now.

Most respondents disagreed with this view, with varying degrees of consideration of that impact.

Not at all	1
Probably	22
Possibly	34
Definitely	54
Don't care	5

Noting the five who just didn't seem to care one way or the other (ambivalence is not resistance I hope), the vast majority answered with a clear 'yes' to this (95 percent).

And the 'winning' belief was that AI will definitely impact project management.

The survey concluded with the question (provocative?): 'Do you think AI will eventually "end" the role of the project manager?'.

Resistance Is Futile 57

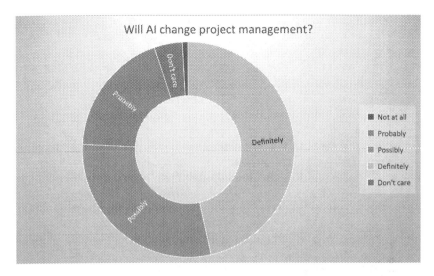

Figure 7.2 Will AI change project management?

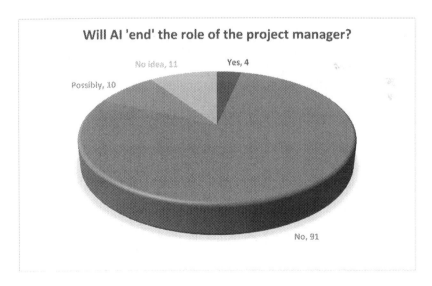

Figure 7.3 Will AI 'end' the role of the project manager?

A small percentage (3 percent) (4 respondents) believed that, indeed, AI would (eventually) remove the need and role of the project manager, and 9 percent (10 respondents) felt that this could possibly be the 'endgame' of the rise of AI into the world of project management.

But 78 percent (91 respondents) felt that there is still a future for project managers (and project management), which I personally never doubted.

As we noted in the opening words of this book:

> Gartner states that by 2030 – so we are not talking too far ahead, only ten years – 80% of the work of today's project managers will be eliminated as AI takes on functions such as data collection, tracking, reporting, analytics, and predictive analysis.
>
> 80% of what you do as project managers today – or what your project managers do if you are head of a PMO or head of a programme, or project practice – 80% of that work will just not be there anymore; it will be eliminated because AI will take it on, and deal with it, and deal with it no doubt in a very consistent and better manner.

Your Virtual Partner

PwC's 'A Virtual Partnership? How Artificial Intelligence Will Disrupt Project Management and Change the Role of Project Managers'[2] provides the following thoughts about whether AI will replace project managers and what project managers' correct attitude towards AI should be:

> Project managers need to capitalise on the opportunities generated by technological disruption, and in many ways be the champions of new technologies as they emerge.
>
> [...]
>
> Both AI and project managers depend on each other; the project manager is required to have the right skill set to be able to manage AI and AI is inoperative without the input and added value of a skilled project manager.

This report further makes some well-considered predictions for the future digital (AI) world of business change:

> Where humans and AI work together, project managers will need to build a skill set that focuses on the areas where AI falls short: these are the core 'people skills' or '21st century skills'. The use of AI will also require a diverse and flexible skill set to be able to cope with future challenges.

It has always been essential for project leaders to have strong communication, negotiation skills and, more popularly accepted these days, emotional intelligence to inspire teams and lead them in a collaboratively productive manner.

In the latest PMI[3] 'Pulse of the Profession' report,[4] the most commonly cited new skills for organisations are soft skills at 45 percent, and this is as true for the project management professional as any other business role, perhaps even more so as the success of each project manager is (almost) wholly dependent on the people in their teams.

Alongside these people (or soft) skills, PwC recommends that we consider the following advice:

> AI acts as a project management's 'virtual partner'; project leaders must have an innovative mindset and customise their knowledge to drive this digital transformation forward. Having strong 'digital know-how' and data science skills is key, alongside security and privacy knowledge.[5]

The 'Global Survey on Artificial Intelligence Impact in Project Management 2020'[6] conducted by PwC Romania and the International Project Management Association (IPMA[7]) found that:

> 52% of project management professionals see the emergence of Digital Assistant role and the adoption of Artificial Intelligence in their profession in the next five years. The roles most likely to be taken over by AI in project management over the next five years are Project manager assistant (52%) and Project manager adviser (44%). More than half of project managers estimate an acceleration of the digitization process in the business environment by implementing artificial intelligence (AI) solutions, from digital assistants to standalone solutions that produce profound changes in the way we perceive and use technology.

As to how and where this AI impact will be most productive, the report declared: 'The three main reasons for adopting AI technologies in project management, indicated by respondents, are: increased productivity (53 percent), improved decisions (52 percent) and increased performance (51 percent)'.

According to Tim Stobierski:[8] 'By automating low value-add tasks, project managers can focus their efforts and energy on completing tasks that most greatly benefit their organization, allowing them to effect greater change and increase the likelihood of achieving the strategic goals of each project'.

As 'agents of change', then, it should come as no real surprise that project managers should be open to change in their own profession and business world, which is just as well as the rise of AI in project management will bring about a huge change, but not a meteor-landing dinosaur-like extinction of the species known as 'project managers'.

But You Need to Change That Mindset

The PMI Pulse of the Profession report, 'AI Innovators: Cracking the Code on Project Management',[9] declares that 'AI isn't the next best thing in a far-off future'; I agree with that, 100 percent. PMI continues: 'Capturing the value of AI isn't just about rolling out a bunch of new technologies. It takes the right people with the right skills and the right attitude'.

PMI talks about the need for a high project management technology quotient, or PMTQ, to be successful in this new AI project world. It describes PMTQ as being defined by three essential traits:

1. Always-on curiosity: Looking for emerging project delivery practices without chasing after every new digital trend.
2. All-inclusive leadership: Getting the best out of your teams, whether they're human or machine.
3. A future-proof talent pool: Recruiting the right people with the mindset to keep current and keep learning while helping their teammates do the same.

You can read more on this in the PMI publication 'The Future of Work: Leading the Way with PMTQ'.[10]

IPMA's report results cited earlier in the chapter noted that while confirming that AI adoption is very much about the tools, it is also as much about changing attitude: 'The transition to artificial intelligence solutions has significant effects, in most companies, involving changes in the transformation of current internal processes and the creation of new ways in which people with different abilities will work with new technologies'.

So, it seems that we can embrace the future (as opposed to trying to resist and fail) but we will have to adjust our thinking somewhat in order to be successful in the adoption of AI in project management.

> It may be hard for an egg to turn into a bird: it would be a jolly sight harder for it to learn to fly while remaining an egg.
>
> (C.S. Lewis)

Which brings us back to the people, of course.
People deliver projects, as we will explore in the next chapter.

Notes

1 The Vogons are a fictional alien race from the planet Vogsphere in *The Hitchhiker's Guide to the Galaxy* who are responsible for the destruction of the Earth, in order to facilitate an intergalactic highway construction project for a hyperspace express route.
2 PwC, 'A virtual partnership? How artificial intelligence will disrupt project management and change the role of project managers', 2019. www.pwc.com/m1/en/publications/virtual-partnership-artificial-ntelligence-disrupt-project-management-change-role-project-managers.html.
3 PMI, the Project Management Institute, is an American nonprofit professional organisation for project management.
4 PMI, 'Pulse of the Profession 2021'. www.pmi.org/learning/thought-leadership/pulse
5 PwC, 'A virtual partnership? How artificial intelligence will disrupt project management and change the role of project managers', 2019. www.pwc.com/m1/en/publications/documents/virtual-partnership-artificial-ntelligence-disrupt-project-management-change-role-project-managers-final.pdf
6 IPMA, 'Report: More than half of project management professionals see the adoption of Artificial Intelligence in their profession in the next 5 years', 15 January 2021. www.ipma.world/report-more-than-half-of-project-management-professionals-see-the-adoption-of-artificial-intelligence-in-their-profession-in-the-next-5-years/
7 The International Project Management Association (IPMA) is a federation of around 70 member associations across the globe, providing qualification standards for individuals working in project, programme, and portfolio management.
8 Tim Stobierski, '6 Project management trends emerging in 2021'. Northeastern University graduate blog, 8 July 2020. www.northeastern.edu/graduate/blog/project-management-trends/
9 PMI, 'AI innovators: Cracking the code on project management', 2019. www.pmi.org/-/media/pmi/documents/public/pdf/learning/thought-leadership/pulse/ai-innovators-cracking-the-code-project-performance.pdf
10 PMI, 'The future of work: Leading the way with PMTQ', 2019. www.pmi.org/learning/thought-leadership/pulse/pulse-of-the-profession-2019

Thoughts from the Real World:

> 'AI will only add to laziness, clumsiness, and poor project performance. The difference between good and bad project managers is the ability to identify and seize opportunity'.

> 'AI will make some things easy and will automate routine tasks – but it will not solve dilemmas and it will not replace a human any time soon'.

Chapter 8

Projects Are About People

Three Big Asks

With regard to the overall AI and project management issues, then we should ask ourselves three big questions:

- What are the project managers of the immediate future going to do?
- Regarding the application of time freed by AI dealing with 80 percent of current tasks, how will project managers focus their efforts?
- And what is the next (in addition to, and empowered by, AI) quantum leap in project success?

The answer to all three is simple, and it is how we concluded the preceding chapter – People deliver projects.

So, I believe, project managers in the 'new AI normal' world will:

- Use all of that AI insight and predictive capability and re-align their day-by-day efforts in the direction of people.
- As such, that amazing 80 percent saving of effort provided by the intelligent application of AI will free up project managers to really get to grips with the complexities of people and teams.
- And yes, this is the next quantum leap in project success: building and leading incredible project teams, anywhere and everywhere that they are individually located, into a single purpose-driven powerhouse.

Having led some of the largest PMOs in the world,[1] I clearly recognise the value gap of the almost untouched area of project team performance management, which I believe will be the next quantum leap in project success.

It is about ensuring greater alignment amongst project team members, knowing that projects are about people, and people (teams) deliver project success.

DOI: 10.4324/9781003175063-8

Project Team Analytics

Project team performance is a critical investment for any organisation which wishes to thrive in the 'new normal' project-based economy and truly optimise the AI-driven project world.[2]

For decades, project management executives and practitioners have been asking the multi-million, and sometimes multi-billion-dollar, question: why did the project fail?

Whatever your definition may be for project success, it is never an easy task getting there. High project failure rates are nothing new and have been well documented. However, when project professionals seek answers to this question, they naturally turn back to the original project plan to identify flaws, be it the estimation, the requirements, or perhaps the business case. Yet there is one place where most don't look for the answers.

The people.

We know that throughout our project life cycle there are a plethora of issues that can arise which can threaten project success. These issues creep up on project managers despite the risk management performed and forecasts put in place; project leaders are constantly investigating where things went wrong, analysing why they did, and strategising how they can be avoided in the future.

Of course, when these exercises are done, the answers are not always found and if they ever are, it is all but too late. This breeds the need for a fresh approach to project performance, an approach which seeks to understand first and foremost those that execute and receive the project plan: the people.

This approach should be a holistic one where all likelihoods are evaluated, and bias is removed, and it should be proactive and less reactive, less periodic, and more real time. This the real true opportunity that AI offers our profession: the chance to get back to what we should be doing – leading great project teams and drawing the best out of people.

Not too long ago, I was at one of the major project management conferences in Europe, which was focused on PMOs, actually. And during one of the breaks, after I completed my keynote presentation in the morning, I was talking to a number of people, as you do at these conferences – networking and all that.

One conversation I had in particular was with a gentleman of a similar age to myself.

We were left alone at one of those coffee tables that you stand up at in conferences, and you know there's never enough room for drinks and food etc., but we were talking to each other and we reflected: 'How was it that we survived in the early days of being project managers, the time when we didn't even realise we were project managers?'

We reflected the fact that both of us had a remarkably similar sort of experience in that it was a number of years before we realised we were acting as project managers, and it was a number of years before we were probably even called 'project managers', and certainly a number of years before we were given any form of education in being a project manager.

And yet somehow, in those early days, we survived.

The conclusion that we both came to was the fact that, while we did not understand what you might call the 'mechanics' of project management – the kind of hard process steps, the methodology, however you want to describe it – we didn't understand that, because no one had taught us that; we were instead, by default, relying on the skills that we did have.

And these skills were predominantly people-oriented skills.

By focusing on the people, we were reasonably successful, moderately successful, sometimes a little unsuccessful I will be honest, but always learning important lessons. But the key thing was that we survived. We both survived in those early years, and it is because of that balance of capability of skills in the area of people. We were pretty convinced that's the case anyway.

Now, certainly in later years, when we were both educated in the process, the method, the mechanics, or however you want to describe it, in project management it certainly helped us; it was certainly a huge benefit to understand the things that I had been doing okay and things I could certainly do better and some things I had not been doing at all. And it definitely made me a better project manager. But I think, on reflection, the industry and the profession has gone a little too far into the process side of things, and less into the area of the people. Even, I would argue, in the area of agile project management, it's significantly better I feel, and the fact is this technique encourages the kind of close interaction with people, but still, still there isn't the true level of focus that's required.

The Opportunity of AI

This brings us back to the opportunity that AI offers us in our profession right now: to take away the burdensome or the onerous tasks, to remove the stuff we don't really like doing, where some intelligence like AI could actually do better than us anyway. Never tiring, greater predictive capabilities, processing huge amounts of data, etc.

It will allow us to free up our time, back to that 80 percent that Gartner said will be released by AI. We will be able to spend our time interacting, leading, and working with the people on our project team, wherever they are in the world. This is the quantum leap; this is the opportunity that will allow the truth that projects are about people to become a reality.

AI in project management will permit project managers, project leaders, and change agents to spend time working with people to really get the best out of them. This thought fits well with Daniel Pink's[3] view on motivation, and something I personally explored in my book, *The Social Project Manager*.[4]

> In 'Drive: The Surprising Truth About What Motivates Us' Pink explains that everything we think we might know about what motivates us is probably wrong.
>
> He puts forward a core concept of motivation called the 4 Ts; in which people want autonomy over their 'Tasks', over their 'Time', over their 'Team', and also through their 'Technique'.
>
> The absence by design or other of this autonomy has bad consequences for performance and motivation. And conversely of course if you want maximum motivation then you have to give people the 4 Ts.
>
> Looking at the 4 Ts we might perhaps conclude that there is little that even a social project manager can do in two of these – 'Tasks' and Time' – and perhaps that is correct but an open channel of communication within the team in even these areas might offer up alternative thoughts that might be beneficial to the team and the work objectives.

This is the 'sandpit' for AI, surely: tasks, time, analytics, and predictive insights.

> But in the other two – 'Team' and 'Technique' – there is ample room for social tool driven benefit. Tools and social media can allow for greater engagement 'within', 'around' and 'about' the project which leads to greater team performance and engagement.
>
> And as far as technique is concerned it is the manager's role to advise on the 'what', but it is the subject matter expert's role to define the 'how', and here again social tools and media can add to this through greater speed of information exchange, higher levels of engagement and wider validation of what is 'best' in each situation.[5]

Under the 'Team' and 'Technique' headings this is where the AI-supported future project manager will thrive.

High-performing teams deliver high-performing projects and, by default of this, great success.

Perfect Symbiosis

Let me put one further argument forward that AI will aid this people-focused approach that project management truly needs.

I was a happy contributor to a short book(let) entitled *Will AI Change the Way You Manage Change?* sponsored by Sharktower.[6] This is well worth a read and you can access the pdf through the link at the end of this chapter.

Just picking on three points of contribution:

'AI can spot problems earlier and drive better decisions', says David Porter, MD, Endeavour Programme. He continues: 'Artificial Intelligence (AI) and machine learning (ML) offer to make a fundamental difference in how projects run. AI does not suffer from optimism bias and it can derive meaning from complex data faster, and at a far greater scale than humans working with traditional project management software tools.'

Claudio Truzzi, Technology Transfer Professional – Digital Innovation, Universite libre de Bruxelles, explains this further: 'AI Systems level the playing field for decision makers'.

How does it do this? Well, 'When faced with complex situations or large amounts of data, people often filter information through biases that prevent them from deriving the most business value from the data'.

And he identifies four types of this 'bias':

> Confirmation bias. People subconsciously select the information that confirms their beliefs and strategically ignore data that challenges their beliefs.
>
> Reality denial. People build an understanding of a situation, and then use various techniques to rationalise away contradictory information.
>
> Availability bias. Not having time to research a situation in depth, people tend to fall back on the most recent information they have.
>
> Experience bias. Experienced people confronting a new problem may see similarities to other situations that they have dealt with in the past. They apply an old solution pattern similar to what they are seeing without taking the time to determine whether new data suggests taking a different action.

One final 'voice' on this from Susie Palmer-Trew, CEO, University of Northampton Students' Union,[7] who states in the Sharktower report: 'To improve project outcomes, bring people and data closer together.'

How does she propose this is possible? 'People are at the heart of project delivery' (well that I agree with 100 percent as this very chapter proves).

> Project delivery, in turn, depends on those people having the rights skills, capacity, information, freedom, and time to fulfill project demand. Projects always start with the best intentions, with everybody pulling in the same direction. Then, new ideas come up, hindsight kicks in, and relationships begin to develop amongst people.

> Often, projects begin to spiral out of control because people do not know how to draw insight from relevant data. They do not know how to bring data close enough to their decision-making process to benefit from it.

Martin Parlett, Head of Programme Management in the Government of Montserrat, commented in the Sharktower report with a word of warning:

> Quality attendance to the human dimensions of change is so much more important. How can we transform our projects into meaningful and inspirational human stories of impact? How can we consistently leverage emotional intelligence to connect and enliven our stakeholders and inform our governance? How can we preference pragmatism and behavioural acuity over unchanging systems and process? AI may have its place for analytics – but it is only as good as the human inputs it receives. As with all tooling, let us get the fundamentals right before grabbing a shiny object/system/software that may end up subduing those important instincts.

Summarising all this, then, bringing people and data together in harmony and alignment is critical to project success. People, through a combination of capability, competence, and time struggle to do this well with the reality of the volume of data potentially available to them. And even if they can achieve this, then it is all derailed by the very human nature of optimism bias.

AI can deal with this in a non-subjective, 'eat as much' as you like, data volumes way. Project managers, who are people, are good at working with, leading, inspiring, and caring about people, and creating those 'stories' of impact.

> In the real-world high-quality project managers are not people who understand and apply the latest sophisticated planning tools. Instead, they are men and women who have the judgment and experience to manage conflicting stakeholders' aims and objectives and act effectively in the face of a constant stream of unpredictable problems.[8]

Project managers need AI, and AI needs human project managers.

To me, this all seems to be perfect in its 'symbiotic relationship'[9] and frees the project manager to work with the people.

Long live the future, where projects really are about people.

Notes

1 I am talking global in reach, hundreds of project managers, thousands of projects – exciting stuff!
2 There will be a new book published by Routledge in 2022 on this very topic – *Project Team Performance: The Missing Piece to Project Success*, which will dramatically increase the probability of project success. In this book, the authors (Taylor and Goldman) will explore a new approach to project success, the continuous process of enabling and empowering teams to reach the optimal levels of performance.
3 Daniel H. Pink is the author of six provocative books about business and human behavior. His books include the long-running New York Times bestsellers *When* and *A Whole New Mind* – as well as the number-one New York Times bestsellers *Drive* and *To Sell Is Human*.
4 Peter Taylor, *The Social Project Manager: Balancing Collaboration with Centralised Control in a Project Driven World*. Routledge, 2015, p. 111.
5 Peter Taylor, *The Social Project Manager: Balancing Collaboration with Centralised Control in a Project Driven World*. Routledge, 2015, pp. 111–112.
6 If you'd like to read this eBook, please use this link: https://uk.sharktower.com/download-7-experts-ebook
7 I should note that Susie Palmer-Trew is co-author with myself on an earlier Routledge book: *Project Management: It's all Bollocks! The Complete Exposure of the World of, and the Value of, Project Management*. Routledge, 2020.
8 Shared by Thomas Walenta, quoting from Tim Brady, Andrew Davies, and Paul Nightingale, 'Dealing with uncertainty in complex projects: Revisiting Klein and Meckling'. *International Journal of Managing Projects in Business*, 7 September 2012. 'www.emerald.com/insight/content/doi/10.1108/17538371211269022/full/html
9 Yes, I realise that machine and humankind is not a true symbiotic relationship, but you get what I mean, I hope.

Thoughts from the Real World:

'The nature of people seems to create a permanent need for project managers to organize their good intentions and keep people and teams moving forward'.

'AI will improve the quality of products in our future. We should definitely be excited about it and willing to learn to deal with our new "teammate"'.

Chapter 9

AI and the Lazy Project Manager

Keep It Simple

In 2009, I wrote, as part of the introduction to my first book (still the most popular and successful one[1]), *The Lazy Project Manager: How to be twice as productive and still leave the office early*, the following:

> Productive laziness is all about success, but success with far less effort.
>
> By advocating being a 'lazy' project manager, I do not intend that we should all do absolutely nothing. I am not saying we should all sit around drinking coffee, reading good books, and engaging in idle gossip whilst watching the project hours go by and the non-delivered project milestones disappear over the horizon. That would obviously be just plain stupid and would result in an extremely short career in project management – in fact, probably in a very short career, full stop!
>
> Lazy does not mean stupid.
>
> No, I really mean that we should all adopt a more focused approach to project management and exercise our efforts where it really matters, rather than rushing around like busy, busy bees involving ourselves in unimportant, non-critical activities that others can better address, or which do not need addressing at all in some cases.
>
> Welcome to the home of 'productive laziness'.[2]

The essence of this vastly different book on project management was that a good project manager would always work 'smarter and not harder' and I tried to present this argument through the use of dinosaur analogies, referencing the work of an Italian economist and a management thinker, weaved in with a touch of the approach of a Prussian field marshall and a beloved Disney character. You know, all the usual stuff!

DOI: 10.4324/9781003175063-9

Since then, I have written and presented a lot. On many different subjects. But always, at least I have always tried, by applying that greatest of principles, 'KISS',[3] to ensure simplicity of purpose, focus, process, and outcome.

And, if you think about it, the rise of support that AI will bring to project management can only be considered as part of this KISS application.

Personally, and I'm quite sure most project managers would agree: sign me up to anything that can alleviate some of the repetitive and arduous (but important of course) tracking, analytics, and reporting activities, and not only alleviate but improve them.

Going for an AI Drive

Let's think about this as a car analogy.

For example, in fact I'm going to explore with you two examples here. In the first, think about travelling in London, which is my nearest city. Now London is a complicated landscape to try and navigate around if you don't know exactly where you're going and even then, there are challenges of traffic congestion, roadworks, road closures, diversions, events, things like that. So, moving around London, assuming you're talking about moving above ground at this point (not using the London Underground), I could get in my car and I could drive to London. I can do that; I have a reasonable knowledge of London, but normally I would not because normally I would catch a train to London and then to get across London it is a matter of choosing one of the famous London taxis, or perhaps or doing a private hire.

Now the advantage of London taxis has always been that the drivers have undertaken, well before they can get into a car, before they can drive a taxi, before they can get their licence, they must undertake something that is known as 'The Knowledge'.[4] The Knowledge is an extremely robust process of evaluating an individual's awareness of road connections, appropriate journeys, alternative routes, etc. And if you ever go to London, you might see a number of people riding around on scooters, with a clipboard mounted on the handlebars, identifying, or trying to learn, what's known as the knowledge of London; it's a very tough thing.

Once you have that knowledge, then, then you know London, you know the way to get around London, you know the most effective routes, the alternative routes, the back roads. If you have ever been in a London taxi, sometimes they take you on some of the most incredible little journeys as they cut through side streets to get to a major location.

Well, you know, that is an incredibly powerful thing.

But if you're talking about, say, Joe Public (myself included), driving along in London, not having passed 'The Knowledge', then this is where you can use some technology such as 'Waze'[5] (other providers are available; this is just my personal favourite).

I'm a heavy user of Waze because of what it can do for the private hire car, or for the delivery driver, or even for the general public who is just getting into their car and going to a place for the first time. It can offer up some incredibly significant opportunities to find the most appropriate route, and it's based on collaborative power.

It is AI empowered in the background with algorithms running to try and constantly find you the best current route, based on information on road layout, understanding of major roadworks that are recorded, but also based on the feedback from all of the other little 'Wazers'[6] out there who are constantly updating that information, providing real-time information that will aid you in your journey and vice versa.

Here we now have the ability to navigate somewhere you don't really know very well and not having to worry about the fact that you're having to try and find the right route. You know, the days when I used to try and drive with a giant map on the passenger seat or having to almost rehearse and memorise new routes. That is long gone: you can just wake up and go and find the most appropriate route by just putting in your desired end location and perhaps some settings (do you want to go on motorways/freeways or do you want to use the back roads etc.). This frees you up to concentrate on what you're supposed to be doing, which is driving a car safely.

In the back of a taxi, I am already allocating the responsibility of safe navigation to someone else, the taxi driver, and by using some navigation technology in my own car then I can also focus away from the distraction of navigation. But there is much more to come.

Inevitably, we will rapidly move towards self-managing cars (The Knowledge will, sadly, one day, die out completely; an incredibly old and very important skill will be tech superseded). In the autonomous vehicles of tomorrow (well they exist now but tomorrow for the general public), then our process, or responsibility, is reduced only to doing what we want to do while in that car; and in the end, all of the technology of AI allows that car to self-manage itself to take you from your starting point 'A' safely on to your journey's end, point 'B'. And all your job is to just enjoy that experience and work or relax, using the in-car entertainment or whatever you wish really. You are fundamentally absolved from (almost) any responsibility as to the safe driving of the vehicle from point A to point B.

Now, some of us might miss that driving experience but I think it's something that we just have to accept will come eventually.

So, to project management, it is very much like this, I think. You know, we are not going to go all the way towards the autonomous project management experience (my opinion). I just cannot see that. But there is a significant step forward in the coming months and years that will take us to a completely different place as far as project management is concerned and, I believe this: it truly fits with the principles that I had all those years ago.

Behind the 'Lazy Project Manager' and the whole 'working smarter not harder' approach I advocate, and the power of working with people (that I believe project management is really all about, managing yourself and managing other people, while delivering a project successfully), then I can only welcome AI into my profession.

I believe AI can only make things better here.

So, here is to the next generation of AI-empowered Lazy Project Managers.

Keep On Being 'Lazy'

I concluded *The Lazy Project Manager* by reminding readers that: 'Progress isn't made by early risers. It's made by lazy men trying to find easier ways to do something'.[7]

The Lazy Project Manager was built for the AI-empowered project management world by using technology to find the easiest way to do something and to spend the freed-up time on focusing on people.

Because people deliver projects.

People!

Notes

1 Until this one perhaps?
2 Peter Taylor, *The Lazy Project Manager: How to be twice as productive and still leave the office early*. Infinite Ideas Limited, 2015, p. 3.
3 KISS, an acronym for 'keep it simple, stupid', is a design principle noted by the U.S. Navy in 1960. The KISS principle states that most systems work best if they are kept simple rather than made complicated; therefore, simplicity should be a key goal in design, and unnecessary complexity should be avoided. The phrase has been associated with aircraft engineer Kelly Johnson. Variations on the phrase include: 'Keep it simple, silly', 'keep it short and simple', 'keep it simple and straightforward', and 'keep it small and simple'.
4 The London taxicab driver is required to be able to decide routes immediately in response to a passenger's request or traffic conditions, rather than stopping to look at a map, relying on satellite navigation or asking a controller by radio. Consequently, the 'Knowledge of London' is the in-depth study of a number of pre-set London street routes and all places of interest that taxicab drivers in that city must complete to obtain a licence to operate a black cab. It was initiated in 1865 and has changed little since. It is the world's most demanding training course for taxicab drivers, and, to pass, applicants will usually need to pass at least 12 'appearances' (periodical one-on-one oral examinations

undertaken throughout the qualification process), with the whole process usually averaging 34 months.
5   Waze is a GPS navigation software app and a subsidiary of Google. It works on smartphones and tablet computers that have GPS support. It provides turn-by-turn navigation information and user-submitted travel times and route details, while downloading location-dependent information over a mobile telephone network.
6   These are the users of Waze who can passively use the system or interact and provide traffic alerts.
7   Robert Heinlein, *Time Enough For Love* US science fiction author (1907–1988) – and yes, a quote of its time, so please replace 'men' with 'people'. Robert Heinlein, *Time Enough For Love*. Ace Books, 1973, p. 169.

Thoughts from the Real World:

> 'It is way too early to be thinking about the application of artificial intelligence in the project management world'.

> 'I can only believe that AI will be a bonus for every serious project manager out there; these are exciting times'.

Chapter 10

A Perspective from the Old and the Wise

Peter: *In this chapter, the first of two companion or balancing ones, I wanted to hear the thoughts of someone who had been there, done that, did some more on top of that, and had been at the forefront of the project management profession. Only one name was in my mind for this: Mr. PMP himself, Lee R. Lambert – Founder of PMP, PMI Fellow, and active in project management for 53 years (and counting).*

Let's see what Lee thinks about this (not so) new-fangled thing, AI, and the impact that it will have on project management.

Illusion Confusion

It all started in 1966 in Salt Lake City, Utah when I began what would later become my project management career, working at Chicago Bridge & Iron in 1966. This initial experience in the working world taught me an unbelievably valuable lesson: things aren't always what they seem!

For example, my new company was not in Chicago; it did not specialise in building bridges and had never worked with iron. The company name created an 'illusion confusion' completely devoid of reality.

Chicago Bridge & Iron was successful as a result of its design and construction of complex, large-diameter, double-walled, cryogenic liquid storage tanks. Not exactly cutting-edge technology, but I was able to master the use of *Smoley's Parallel Tables of Logarithms and Squares*.[1] Without knowing it at the time, this extensive 'manual' use of trigonometry functions in doing my everyday calculations for designing tanks was preparing me for an epiphany that would come later.

Seven years later when I first starting hearing about this new concept called artificial intelligence (AI), I felt like it very well could be another of those 'illusion confusions' created by its name alone. After all, there is nothing artificial in artificial intelligence. There should be no confusion – it is REAL! But it requires careful planning and transformation of existing project information to realise valuable intelligence in

DOI: 10.4324/9781003175063-10

support of the project decision-making process. The fact is that it has been proven that when AI is correctly used by the recipient, it will result in substantial value add on any project.

More than 20 years after starting my first job in SLC, my interest in AI became more pronounced when IBM's Deep Blue supercomputer,[2] capitalising on the application of AI and its sophisticated use of algorithms, defeated Garry Kasparov to become the World Champion of Chess. It didn't seem possible, but a COMPUTER was the World Champion! After that highly publicised chess match, the world could no longer ignore the fact that AI was real and that its potential uses were essentially unlimited.

At the time, I was responsible for the implementation of a Department of Energy Earned Value Management System[3] (EVMS) for General Electric's Breeder Reactor Division in Sunnyvale, California. This was a project valued at more than $300 million USD per year and the requirement to use EVMS presented a perfect opportunity to capitalise on the power of AI concepts to extrapolate historical project data to accurately forecast numbers that would predict the future status of a project. That indisputable fact associated with forecasting the future is recognised as one of the most valuable aspects of EVMS. It has proven its ability to accurately predict the future based on the past. I believe in not making the same mistake twice and I have religiously maintained that 'whatever has happened in the past will continue to happen in the future, unless someone does something about it!'

On my projects that 'someone' is ME!

Actionable Information

AI presented a great opportunity to extrapolate large volumes of historical data. This EVMS forecasting had been a strength of the methodology for years, but until the application of AI techniques the determination of the future conditions had been the result of an arduous and labour-intensive effort. It was so challenging that it was usually only done monthly. But then the product of the manual effort had no resemblance to 'real-time' reporting. Now, with the availability and utilisation of AI, this foundation for making informed project decisions affecting future performance could be accomplished with flexibility, sophistication, and speed.

I must confess that in the years since the start of my career in project management (1966), I had 'invented' my own AI term and it has become a mainstay in my approach to managing projects. My AI stands for Actionable Information. My position has long been that the reason 'bad' decisions are made on projects is primarily due to inadequate, incomplete, and/or lack of availability of decision support information that represents the actual current and future (projected) status of the project.

My almost maniacal demand that AI be planned and used throughout the life cycle of a project has resulted in a continuum of successful projects.

No matter whose definition of AI is being used, the technology that exists today provides every project manager and project team member with the potential to not just predict the future, but actually create it based on the decisions they make. The famous Austrian management consultant Peter Drucker[4] is credited with saying: 'You cannot predict the future, but you can create it!' I passionately believe that using artificial intelligence to produce a different kind of AI (Actionable Information) will result in better and significantly more timely decision making for every project.

In my opinion, the current status of AI provides a unique opportunity to add value in many areas of project management. Some areas will stand to reap more benefits than others so I thought it might be worthwhile to examine those project management efforts where the use of AI should be seriously considered and will yield the most valuable outcome.

Remember, projects are not chess matches, but AI, when used properly, will lead to a 'win' for the project manager who effectively uses it.

No Free Lunch

Using the accepted project management process flow, I will illustrate some of the most beneficial areas where capitalising on AI will be high value add. But it must be understood and remembered that the beneficial use of AI in project management will require frequent iterations throughout a project life cycle and must be carefully integrated with a plethora of other critical organisational information.

According to the Project Management Institute's Megatrends 2021 report,[5] 'AI has surged well beyond the realm of just automating routine tasks'. I agree that AI is clearly an uber-creator of information (data) and its implications are gargantuan when it comes to empowering today's project managers with the ability to make timely 'informed' decisions where only 'best-guess' judgements were made before. But the project manager must not forget that there is 'no free lunch'. In order to capitalise on the power of AI, a substantial investment of time and effort is required to create the AI foundation (planning) that will serve as the springboard for more comprehensively integrated and timely project information in support of the project manager's productive project decisions.

Therein lies the same AI problem that has plagued the project management profession since the beginning of time.

> Fact: AI will *not* replace good planning!
> Fact: AI will *not* make bad planning good.

The project manager and his/her team must accept responsibility for creating a realistic project plan that identifies specific measurable objectives and the resources (human and other) to be used over time to accomplish those objectives. Once this 'project plan' is created and approved, it becomes the project's Performance Measurement Baseline[6] (PMB) and has the associated benefit of machine learning. The contribution of AI throughout the development and execution of the project plan becomes irreplaceable and enables those using it to thoroughly analyse current status, anticipate impacts on future status, and examine anticipated outcomes of potential decisions – *before* they are made.

Additionally, it should be noted that there aren't many project management tools with AI incorporated. In fact, according to Rachel Burger, Capterra analyst:[7] 'Project management has been a field that has been slow to adopt the benefits of machine learning'. However, a recent Gartner report[8] by authors Tom Austin and Mark Hung stated: 'AI will be so ingrained in the workforce that AI integration will be essential by 2021'.

Beneficial Uses of AI in Project Management

Let's now look at some of the most obvious beneficial uses of AI in project management. Project managers must think about the potential power AI bestows upon them.

For example, AI enables the use of information captured from past projects (closeout reports) relative to individual resource productivity rates, accuracy of estimates of time and money, etc. (machine learning). Utilising this valuable historical information and projecting it into the future will result in creating a much more realistic project plan.

One significant problem almost every project manager is confronted with is that we traditionally plan our projects in resource 'effort' hours *but* execute the project in 'duration' hours. In other words, projects are essentially 'behind schedule' the day they begin due to the unrealistic resource allocation planning. This occurs for one simple reason: failure to recognise that in a matrix-driven organisation, the human resources in every resource skill set pool are almost always allocated simultaneously to multiple projects. This overcommitted condition would benefit from the AI ability to rapidly process multiple project plans to detect resources planned to be in 'two or more places at the same time'!

In addition, typically no attention is paid to individual productivity rates based on past performance compared to plan. Unfortunately, eight hours of resource-effort is seldom eight hours of productive duration when the resource is committed to four projects at the same time.

How will using AI solve this problem?

Truth: It won't!

Unless the organisation has committed to comprehensive integrated planning for all projects to be conducted. If the organisation has adopted an integrated planning approach, the use of information generated from each project resource allocation plan can be easily merged to isolate and highlight resource conflicts that will need to be resolved. It does not take a genius to know that there are only 'so many' of one resource skill available to assign to a single project.

But AI concepts can enable the project manager to quickly identify those areas where resource conflicts will have an impact on his/her ability to deliver based on the PMB. AI empowers the project manager to rapidly conduct a 'what if' analysis[9] to determine the impact the identified resource constraints may have on the ability to meet specific project objectives. AI information will facilitate the required negotiations needed to resolve the conflict. Project managers should never fear AI. They can always identify these conflicts manually, but the project will be over before they isolate the problems.

In the world of project management, the availability of specific skill set resources is one of the biggest concerns a project manager has when his/her projects are in direct competition with other projects that share the need for the same skill set. Using AI, the project manager can conduct 'cause and effect' analysis[10] to quantify the impact of resource conflicts, often caused when one resource skill is used to plan, but different resource skill is actually assigned to the execution of the work. This is often jokingly referred to as 'bait and switch' – a technique regularly used in the car sales profession.[11]

Once quantified, an examination to determine the effect on meeting key organisational objectives can be conducted and converted to impacts on organisational business priorities.

The ability to extrapolate and merge resource-related data not only helps the project managers; it is also extremely valuable to the functional/line manager for individual 'resource pool' utilisation. The functional/line manager's performance is based on how effectively he/she manages the resource pool. The objective of a utilisation histogram is for a functional/line manager is to be flat, indicating that all resources have been applied 'all the time'.

Sadly, that objective is not the objective of a project manager, whose utilisation histogram for project resources should match the distribution of resources based on the project plan.

The problem associated with 'body count' resource planning is made even more complex when you consider the matter of individual resource productivity by skill set. All resources are *not* created equal. Not only does the project manager need to worry about getting a resource, he/she must also be concerned that it is the 'right' resource for the specific task to be completed. One of the advantages of using proven AI concepts is to be able to apply several variables to a project situation and be able to rapidly identify the best option. In the case of resource planning, the two critical variables are availability and relative productivity (an output of machine learning) on any identified task.

As stated above, most of our project resource planning is done in Effort hours. But experienced project managers understand that those effort hour estimates need to be converted into duration hours to realistically determine how much actual time must pass before the work can actually be completed.

> For example, if a task is estimated by a Subject Matter Expert (SME) to take 8 effort hours, but the SME is only available 25% of the time, the duration hours for actual linear planning is 32 hours – not 8. But wait, it gets worse. Imagine that the SME that provided the 8-effort hour estimate is not available when the time comes to do the work. The functional/line resource pool owner therefore assigns a substitute resource. However, the newly assigned resource is not a SME and is only 50% as productive as the original SME. Suddenly the duration time needed to complete this task is 64 hours – not 8, not 32.

You can make this calculation for an individual task and isolate time impacts. But doing it for multiple tasks within an integrated PMB to determine possible time impacts, critical path impacts, resource utilisation impacts, financial impacts, etc. requires the capacity and applicability of AI. The importance of this approach to planning is amplified when applied to multiple projects sharing the same resources. Suddenly the conversion of effort hour estimates to duration hours and the impacts of resource productivity rates on task duration is no longer optional. In fact, it should be mandatory.
The formula seems simple:

> Duration hours equal: (Effort Hours/Availability)/Productivity

But when required for an entire project portfolio consisting of dozens of projects and thousands of tasks, the power of automation/merging becomes indispensable. AI facilitates current decision making but it enables the capturing of significant quantities of project data from past projects for use in the future on new and more complex projects. Providing the proper organisational preparation and planning has established the foundation for capitalising on AI.

Some Serious Considerations

While the potential benefits of AI in project management are plentiful, there are two areas that warrant serious consideration.

1. Project Forecasting
2. Project Risk Management

These two areas require the ability to 'look ahead' and have always been dependent upon anticipating the future before it occurs. However, this 'fortune teller' component of project management has always relied on input from 'old timers' with years of applied experience – the been there, done that, got the T-shirt kind of people. Now with the competency that comes with thoughtful utilisation of the AI, even junior project managers can look as though they can see the future. In everyday life we are often amazed by people who say (and some demonstrate the ability) they can predict the future.

With AI *you* can predict the future for your project by exploiting historical performance and creating a window into the future.

One of the strengths of the EVMS approach to project management is its ability to project future status information that can be used to make decisions in the best interest of the project and the organisation. My rule of thumb for projecting current status to represent the future is the project should be 30 percent complete – either time or cost – before the result of the projections are representative of the future. Using the power of AI to facilitate the projections makes it possible to make project decisions that avoid the 'it's too late now' analysis. If 30 percent into the execution of a project you can forecast that, based on historical performance, at completion you will be months late and 25 percent over budget, you now have time to determine what action should be taken to avoid, or minimise, these at-completion variances.

If you have ever been responsible for an EVMS implementation, you will recognise that the opportunity to effectively use this approach is directly dependent upon the ability to automate project information to empower the users to forecast potential outcomes and consider 'what if' analysis to determine the most productive decisions based on those forecasts.

With AI, several alternatives can easily be examined in a matter of hours. Try doing this option investigation manually (I have had the pleasure?) and you will quickly understand why AI can be a significant contributor to project (and organisational) management success.

While the ability to make meaningful and realistic project forecasts is directly dependent upon the quality of the project plan and the actual status of progress compared to that plan, this is not the case for risk management. Risk management is perhaps one of the most critical activities undertaken by a project manager and using AI will greatly increase the value add of executing risk management.

AI will make substantial contributions to the successful use of the traditional risk management model. Using the machine learning answers to questions from past projects, risk event, probability, impact, and risk response can be more realistically determined. Once the anticipated risk probability and impact are determined, the project manager can then perform the 'what if' analysis iterations mentioned above that will serve as input to the risk response decision. Considering all of the project and organisational variables that need to be considered, it would be impossible without AI.

As demonstrated by IBM's Deep Blue computer winning the World Championship of Chess in 1997, the power of AI gave the computer the advantage of analysing the outcome of thousands of potential chess moves before selecting the most beneficial one. With this power of 'prediction', the probability of 'winning' was dramatically improved. Even with AI, Deep Blue only won two matches while losing one and playing to a draw in three. There is no guarantee that AI will lead to success, but like chess, the chances of a successful project are greatly increased through the analysis of multiple variables.

All of this sounded too good to be true for project managers, so I turned to a source with whom I have had the opportunity to work side-by-side in the past, Philip Martin, CEO of Cora Systems.[12]

Martin said: 'Make no mistake, AI is coming into the PPM world. Soon the Cora PPM will be monitoring human or system behaviors and making recommendations for specific courses of action to avoid project risk, overruns, or a schedule faux pas'. Martin also pointed out: 'There is a distinction between machine learning, which uses the existing data to improve performance, and AI, which will predict and suggest corrective action'.

Cora, like many of the companies seeking to capitalise on the growth of AI, is planning to produce a risk report or a project summary report that will determine Red–Amber–Green status automatically. Martin, the Cora CEO, shared: 'I believe the current AI industry is just at the tip of the ice-berg. AI libraries are constantly improving, like the voice recognition software of 10 years ago'.

What Won't AI Do for Project Management?

The purpose of this chapter was to examine the query: 'What can AI do for project management?' After my research and discussions with experts, I am afraid I have to answer that question with a question of my own: 'What won't AI do for project management?'

I want to close by sharing that if I would have had the power of AI available early in my 54-year career[13] I would have ruled the world of project management.

Notes

1 C.K Smoley, *Smoley's Parallel Tables of Logarithms and Squares*. CRC Press 1989.
2 Deep Blue was a chess-playing computer developed by IBM. It was the first computer to win both a chess game and a chess match against a reigning world champion under regular time controls.
3 Earned value management, earned value project management, or earned value performance management is a project management technique for measuring project performance and progress in an objective manner.
4 Peter Ferdinand Drucker was an Austrian management consultant, educator, and author, whose writings contributed to the philosophical and practical foundations of the modern business corporation.
5 PMI, 'Megatrends 2021'. www.pmi.org/learning/thought-leadership/megatrends
6 The Performance Measurement Baseline (PMB) is an important tool in earned value management used by programme managers and systems engineers in the technical assessment process to appraise a programme's technical progress.
7 Rachel Burger, 'I, project manager: The rise of artificial intelligence in the workplace'. Capterra blog, 12 June 2017. https://blog.capterra.com/i-project-manager-the-rise-of-artificial-intelligence-in-the-workplace/
8 Gartner, 'Conversational AI to shake up your technical and business worlds', 2016. www.gartner.com/en/documents/3463317
9 The what-if scenario analysis is a project management process that evaluates different scenarios to predict their effects – both positive and negative – on the project objectives. It also allows project managers to prepare contingency plans in order to overcome the impacts of the unexpected situations.
10 Cause and effect analysis helps you to think through the causes of a problem, including possible root causes, before you start to think of a solution – not just symptoms. By identifying all possible causes and not just the most obvious, you can work towards removing the problem.
11 In a bait and switch, the seller uses their most seasoned professionals to do the sales pitch, but once the contract is signed, the seller assigns much more junior staff to actually perform the work.
12 Cora is an international provider for project portfolio management (PPM) based in Dublin, Ireland. https://corasystems.com/
13 With many more to come – Peter.

Thoughts from the Real World:

> 'Large portions of this technology will be deployed in the next 1–2 years on the basis of cost-cutting initiatives. Realization of the true potential will come later'.

> 'We are already 'behind the curve' on understanding what AI can do for project management'.

Chapter 11

A Perspective from the Young and Enthusiastic

Peter: And now, in the second of the two companion or balancing chapters of viewpoints from either end of the career spectrum, we hear the voice of a young project professional to learn how they feel AI will impact their chosen profession in the future.

I was delighted to persuade Marco Steidel to contribute, after we had worked together on a highly popular PMI Germany sponsored 'AI in PM workshop' in 2020. Marco is going to talk to us about AI through the eyes of a Digital Native.

Hope and Fear!

AI is a technology innovation that causes both fear and hope in humans at the same time.

This apparent contradiction and conflict arises from, on the one hand, the inherent human nature of making use of innovations and fostering change that improves and protects our lives against, on the other hand, the equally human in-built protective characteristic that new technology innovations can harm us or can be potentially used against us in the wrong hands.

There is continuous change and progress in the development of new technologies and in the way of thinking. Or, in the words of the Greek philosopher Heraclitus:[1] 'The only constant in life is change'. By nature, this happens to our planet constantly and we call this evolution.

Evolution in nature and the change to our lives caused by development in technology invented by ourselves will continue and never stop. It depends on us, human society, as to how well we will make use of the opportunities to adopt such change for good through the definition and establishment of smart, simple, and well-understood sets of ethical rules and guidelines that try to prevent any misuse of technology by us or by others against ourselves.

DOI: 10.4324/9781003175063-11

Digital Natives

From the perspective of a project manager who belongs by definition to the Generation-Y[2] social group, which is seen as the first generation that grew up using digital components during their childhood, I can be termed as a Digital Native.

A Digital Native can be seen as a person who is able to make use of knowledge and technology in combining traditional well-established channels by extending them through digital channels of expertise to explore new methods and new knowledge, and save time in doing whatever needs to be done. In other words, a Digital Native is ready and open to explore new tools and methods that help them to do an activity in a simpler manner, and in less time than was required to invest before.

Besides the cognitive stimulation of Digital Natives using innovative technologies and digital media while growing up, and later making use of them in their private and professional lives, the saving of time leads to a new cognitive infrastructure in the way of thinking and acting in digital fast lanes. Such 'fast lanes' open the doors to opportunities to combine traditional methods with new capabilities and foster change, and will lead to disruption in many aspects within our society. This change process is one of the characteristics of the current digital era, called 'Digital Transformation',[3] which has just begun and will continue for an indefinite period of time until the next-big-thing innovation appears on the horizon. It is, therefore, essential for all of us to help each other to transform our society by bringing down the walls of a focused mindset in establishing a growth mindset, which will enable us to harness the opportunities that are waiting to be explored by us.

As a project manager of the younger generation, there is already widespread working practice in environments mainly based and influenced by the Lean management[4] approach in combination with several agile frameworks and methodologies. The main goal of these approaches is to optimise processes, quality, and output and, last but not least, to try to avoid waste as much as possible.

In times marked by a lack of having the right resource with the right skillset available on site in time, it becomes even more critical to make use of technology that helps us to progress with our endeavour as far as possible. Although we still hope to hire the best candidate soon, even with the right candidate it is becoming increasingly important to also have the right tools in place, which allow us to analyse the massive amount of project data in a way that minimises the risk of failure while at the same time optimising the quality in output within a shorter period of time and, if possible, with fewer costs.

Regardless of generation, every project manager has to constantly deal with this magical triangle of scope, schedule, and costs, focusing on quality at its centre.

Smart People Need Smart Tools

To make use of the massive amount of data available, smart people require smart tools to make use of the opportunity to successfully achieve their targets.

For success in the near and long-term future, it is time to think about methods and strategies for how AI solutions could help every type of manager in grouping, analysing, understanding, and interpreting the data. The data may also provide recommendations for next-action items to be in the position to make better decisions, leading to better outcomes for the project, the organisation with its employees, and ideally also for the society and environment we all live in.

Sustainability plays a vital role in making use of AI solutions because these solutions not only help us to improve our lives; they also require time to get trained by us and in the next step to learn from us through different algorithms. This latter step enables achievement of a level of trust in situations where we as humans are looking for information that supports our thoughts or for recommendations on how we can do something better or differently to avoid waste and failures before they become apparent.

AI solutions require study time in the beginning and during operation before they can provide us with their hoped-for value. Otherwise, they will never achieve the level of trust that is essential for them to become our trusted advisor in every aspect of our life. It can be compared with our own development as a child with the difference that AI solutions do not need around 18 years to become a respected mature adult in our society. Instead, only a few months after their development, this technology is already able to consider and partly understand how we think and how we react and decide in certain situations – simply by monitoring us and analysing our reaction based on the data and the data flow we produce.

How long it will take until these tools create real value for us depends on many influencing factors, such as the people, guidelines, laws, development in technology, environment, and complexity. But one thing is for sure: however much time it takes, an initial improvement, although only a tiny one without significant impact yet, can be seen after the technology has been implemented over the first few months. Steady increases in regular quality improvement will see the first few recommendations gaining an increasing amount of impact that can be recognised after just a few months of implementation.

After considering what I have already written, I would like to highlight that AI solutions do not need much time to achieve a level whereby they bring value into our lives to create better value and outcomes in the future.

The field of AI technology offers such a broad space for science, research, and innovative development that our brains can hardly be expected to cope. Making predictions about what future growth this technology offers us, and how we could make use of it in a legal and reasonable manner, is almost impossible but we do need to also consider the risks which might come with this technology. It is a balancing act.

Science Fiction to Science Reality

For those people who are interested in science fiction novels or movies, the expectations that come with AI technologies are probably huge, and parts of it will remain fictional and never become a reality. But looking back into history, science fiction has always influenced our future development and that of the environment we live in, and this will certainly continue both now and in the future.

While the development and acceptance of AI technologies in business environments is still taking its early footsteps, it is vital to discuss, and finally define, guidelines that foster understanding of the technology and acceptance of how and where AI technology is allowed to be used. Misuse of AI solutions or any kind of societal harm need to be avoided as much as possible.

The code of conduct, the development of which is mandatory, should provide a framework of guidelines and boundaries within AI technology that must be followed and respected, but we also have to ask ourselves if redefining new barriers will limit in any way our thinking and limit the development of possible future innovations? Besides this question, the following is also equally important when starting to think about developing or implementing such solutions: To what extent can we build trust in AI solutions and in which fields should we start exploring and gaining first experience in using them?

These are just two examples of many questions that each manager who needs to use IT systems to get his or her daily work done should both consider and be able to answer before commencing an AI project. This brings us to the point of thinking about a strategy for how to start an AI initiative in order to set up a pilot which is meaningful on the one hand and provides value for you to overcome one of your main pain-points within the project, and can also have a secondary impact on your client or the organisation.

First of all, you need to think about present pain-points and make yourself aware of their negative impact on your project and the environment you are in.

Secondly, check your employees' experience and skill profiles within your organisation to become aware of who might be helpful, capable, and willing to find creative solutions through searching for and finding the right data, enabling the required interfaces, and establishing a working process for further analysis.

The Data Jungle

Without having the right people on board to work on your pain-points, it will be hard to find a way out of the data jungle. Therefore, make use of your colleagues, partners, and customers through collaboration and cooperation, and proceed further with the next step in trying to group and prioritise the pain-points and dependent tasks which you would like to either resolve or automate in some way, or where you will require assistance through any type of research or advisory services based on the available data.

Do not be afraid if you are not fully aware of what kind of data is already available and accessible to you within the organisation. Due to the massive amount of data, I would say that nearly none of us are fully aware of the whole data pool within our environment. And this is exactly the point: this is where AI solutions step in to assist us in gaining more clarity about what is going on now, why something is like it is, what might happen next (trends), and how we need to adjust our current environment with its processes and our own behaviour to reduce mistakes and waste in the future.

Regarding what this means for project managers, who are one of the key players in the game to drive the change forward, I like the following words by Paul Boudreau[5] in his summary of the book *Applying Artificial Intelligence to Project Management*:

> Project Managers have a critical role in the adoption of AI tools for Project Management. They will be responsible for the appropriate collection and use of data, as well as the successful integration of AI tools in the new project methodology. Project Managers need to be champions of the true picture of this technology while, at the same time, their activities become the target of change.

As a project manager of the future, you have to develop the right mindset and be open to change and innovation. You should be aware of what tools the market offers you now and not far into the future. Finally, you should be open-minded without having much fear of asking technology and data-based solutions for assistance, or even being guided by them.

The AI Marketplace

While analysing the type of tools the market already offers, you will come across a growing number of startups and a few bigger players which have targeted the group of change drivers (e.g. project and product managers, agile coaches, chief digital officers, business developers, salespeople etc.) as their primary customers for their AI software solutions.

As an example, there are currently many tools that are already helping you in detecting future trends by analysing company internal communication tools like chat and messenger services to collect data about possible risks and constraints like emotional feelings, project tiredness of project members, potential delays in getting certain tasks fulfilled on time due to unstable dependencies with other project-related tasks, and many more. When the data is there, which is indeed already mostly the case, and an AI system has been implemented in a way that is easy to use by non-technically oriented people as well, then every manager who is leading people and is in charge of running the business efficiently, and of developing it further in gaining more market share compared to its competitors, should try to make use of AI systems as their personal digital assistant to unleash the full potential of the organisation.

This would help the manager in analysing future types of personalised key performance indicators (KPIs[6]), such as a person's level of motivation and tiredness, which provides information about the possibility of how likely it is that a person is losing motivation or feels drained when they have to repeatedly perform the same task. In combination with other personalised KPIs like recent performance, the actuality of skills, and the focused interest and availability of the employees a manager is leading, AI systems can assist managers in building and forming the right team while staying focused on the goals to run and complete the prescribed endeavour efficiently, with the right quality within budget and on time.

There is no argument about when AI solutions will be implemented in use cases like this; it is actually a matter of how you want to make use of such AI solutions inside your company in being able to compete with your competitors and maybe always be a little step ahead of them by having a growth mindset and being open to change and innovations like AI-empowered help.

Through this example, we can see that AI does not only apply to products like autonomous machines (e.g. robots and cars) and how they interact and communicate with us through sensors, or to the way manufacturing sites are managed; it also applies and plays a vital role in company leadership too. In relation to this, more and more solutions are being developed and are quickly implemented; it will be exciting to see how quickly the level of acceptance and trust will increase over time in using such digital assistants in our daily business life. It will also be interesting to see how people react when they become aware that the whole team representing a group of the best-suitable candidates who were available at the time has been formed by an algorithm.

In this regard, further research is required in the future to find answers to questions such as: 'Will it drive each individual as part of such a team, as well as the team itself, formed by an AI solution, if people know they are part of an elite group on a mission to success, or will it harm such drive and success in any way'?

Automated Tasks May Not Be AI in Action

Although the above-listed examples belong to AI, we must be careful not to make a mistake in interpreting automated tasks as already being a type of AI system. To elucidate the difference between what is automation and what is AI, please see the following basic examples.

Automation, for instance, in the world of project management, is a system mainly based on automated processes that warn you in the form of notifications as soon as a task is marked as either 'At Risk' or 'On Hold', or when the project becomes overdue. AI is instead a solution based on an algorithm that analyses the data following your previously defined criteria and guidelines; based on the outcome of the analysis, the system warns you or provides a recommendation to you or will advise you. Often, AI systems already operate in combination with automated tasks or use cases in the background, where the AI system adds artificial intelligence to come up with conclusions and recommendations that should provide you with improvements and further development within your value chain.

Returning to strategy, you also should try to establish and make use of a good partnership with your preferred software vendor of AI solutions in thinking about the use cases where you require assistance in creating better value and outcome by an intelligent assistant at your end and for your clients and partners. Software vendors have, in reality, just started the development of suitable solutions, which will become the baseline for further developments. However, for further development in a way that really meets the demands of you, your stakeholders, and the majority of your customers, this always requires feedback from you as the end user to transform the capability of AI solutions into a triple-win solution for ideally all, or at least most, of the parties involved.

What Excites Me?

An example of a possible use case I would be really interested in is a solution that informs you and makes recommendations to you, as the project manager, about events somewhere in the world that might affect your value chain and the project's success in any way.

Imagine you are the responsible project manager working on a globally scaled project where you depend on different supply-chains of material across the world to get your products produced. Would it not be nice and immensely helpful if there was an AI system running in the background that monitors all of your worldwide supply-chains and tracks dependencies on project-related tasks, warning you as soon it recognises somewhere an event that could lead to disruptions by providing you one (or several) recommendation(s) on how to act based on this situation. Or perhaps it has even already made a decision, and commenced action accordingly, based on the experience it already gained to select the best option independently.

I think such a solution would be a great achievement by the software vendors, which would provide benefits in the form of an artificial assistant for every project manager while managing the project.

The COVID-19 pandemic crisis is the most recent example where such a solution would have probably helped many companies find ways to adjust their global supply-chains in time to ensure that no delays or even break-ups in their supply-chains occurred. Many organisations failed to adjust their supply-chains when China was still the only country that suffered from the virus. A few months later, caused by several lockdowns and further spread of the virus, lots of the supply-chains collapsed and needed some time to be rebuild as soon as people were allowed again to get back to work.

AI systems are not magic wizards that could avoid any problem for you, but those solutions can at least limit your endeavour's failure and optimise your risk management in general.

Realistically, even when you have the best AI system in place when such a global pandemic or event happens, and all alternative options to your supply-chain are affected, then even the smartest AI system cannot help, apart from taking care of adjustments of statuses for tasks and projects based on analysing the news it receives from external resources.

Concluding Thoughts

To conclude this discussion on AI from the view of being a Digital Native, I would like to highlight that AI should not be seen as the holy grail, helping us to resolve all of our problems. It also should not be seen in a too sceptical way as the enemy which will overtake us and destroy us someday.

Of course, this is a possibility if we do not carefully consider the definition and strict monitoring of AI ethical guidelines by a global independent authority (as occurs with organisations like the IAEA [International Atomic Energy Agency] for atomic energy).

AI solutions will help us to better understand processes and their data, to be better prepared for incidents we might have overseen before, and will assist us in preparing and making better decisions. Or AI could even act on our behalf automatically, based on the experience and knowledge the system was able to gain through pre-defined guidelines, algorithms, and by monitoring all types of different channels, including us, besides analysing coherences by themselves. AI will help us to resolve some of the problems from the past and present while developing future innovations (e.g. smart robots, autonomous driving and flying), which we can use to build a new future that will probably be more digital and quite different from today.

Let us put our scepticism and fear of AI aside, and let us go for the opportunity it provides, because we as project managers are one of the crucial key-drivers to drive the change for a new tomorrow.

By adopting new technologies like AI, we as project managers have the opportunity to automate and outsource a few of our tasks to our very smart digital assistant through which we are winning time to focus more on other topics like strategy work, business development, and business model innovation, or even our private lives and the society we live in.

As project managers, it is in our hands to make use of the potential of AI in improving sub-categories of project management, such as risk management, and to develop the fields of utilisation while securing the reputation of our future job profile. We will become and act as one of the leaders ensuring success in driving the change in a professional manner through an increasing number of projects. AI solutions will help us to increase the overall success rate of projects while following our goal of becoming one of the organisation's future leaders and strategic thinkers. Therefore, think positive, consider the chances it provides more than the risks, explore, and go for the options it offers, use your opportunity to grow, and, last but not least, have fun in doing your job successfully while creating value for your clients, employer, yourself, and your environment.

I wish you all the best at work with your personal digital assistant based on AI technology.

If you wish, I am looking forward to hearing back from you about how quickly you could adapt yourself and build trust alongside increasing efficiency in using an AI system at work.

Be open to the change and enjoy it.

Notes

1 Heraclitus of Ephesus was an ancient Greek, pre-Socratic, Ionian philosopher and a native of the city of Ephesus, which was then part of the Persian Empire. His appreciation for wordplay and oracular expressions, as well as paradoxical elements in his philosophy, earned him the epithet 'The Obscure' from antiquity.
2 Millennials, also known as Generation Y (or simply Gen Y), are the demographic cohort following Generation X and preceding Generation Z.

Researchers and popular media use the early 1980s as starting birth years and the mid-1990s to early 2000s as ending birth years, with 1981 to 1996 being a widely accepted defining range for the generation. Most millennials are the children of baby boomers and early Gen Xers; millennials are often the parents of Generation Alpha.

3 Digital Transformation is the adoption of digital technology to transform services or businesses, through replacing non-digital or manual processes with digital processes or replacing older digital technology with newer digital technology.

4 The main purpose of Lean management is creating value to the customer by optimising resources. Lean management principles aim to create a stable workflow based on actual customers' demand. Continuous improvement is a major part of Lean management, ensuring that every employee is involved in the process of improvement.

5 Paul Boudreau, *Applying Artificial Intelligence to Project Management*, 2019 (Independently published).

6 A performance indicator or key performance indicator is a type of performance measurement. KPIs evaluate the success of an organisation or of a particular activity in which it engages.

Thoughts from the Real World:

'We really don't actually have a choice in this, it is not a 'take it or leave' option. AI is coming'!

'Project management has, and always will, shape its own future. If the people want AI, the people will get AI. If the powers don't want it, then it will be sidelined for as long as possible to protect the status quo'.

Chapter 12

Thoughts on the Future Project Manager

Five Big (as Yet) Unanswered Questions

This chapter debates five critical questions, which explore the ownership of project delivery, whether we still need qualified and certified project managers, and if we do, will there still be a need for some overarching guidance method or framework process?

In addition, where will the cumulative knowledge of projects and project management reside in the future and, if the full potential of AI project management is fulfilled, then what will that mean for today's project managers?

1. Can anyone 'do' project management in the AI-empowered project world?
2. In the AI project world, will the certifications and qualifications of today be irrelevant?
3. Will methodology be a thing of history when AI enables project managers in the future?
4. Will the project management 'bodies of knowledge' exist in an AI 'cloud' of data-driven 'intelligence' rather than in the current disparate professional bodies?
5. In the AI project world, will the skillset of the project manager be devalued?

Apologies but I do not have all the answers to this; I really don't. I am not sure anyone does.

But let me 'feed the flames' of debate in these five key areas with regard to the future of the project management world when AI takes its inevitable (supportive) role.

DOI: 10.4324/9781003175063-12

In the AI/PM World, Can Anyone 'Do' Project Management?

If AI grabs hold of that 80 percent of what we do right now as project managers, and makes it its very own because it will do it so much better than us humans can, what will that leave?

And will those 'can't be done by AI' actions be of such a simple nature that really anyone will be able to 'do' project management?

It will become a lower-level skillset and could, perhaps, be embedded in normal day-to-day business work?

I have spoken, and written, for quite some time, about the rise of the 'projects as usual' activity inside organisations – the following is from *Project Management: It's All Bollocks!*:

> In my view there are three components of organisational activity these days; business as usual (of course), projects as projects (pure and simple/complex), but also what I refer to as 'projects as usual' (change, managed as part of the daily work of business people who may or may not have 'project manager' in their title or even resume).[1]

Perhaps what we will see is a bi-directional outcome.

One path is that those who lead 'projects as projects' will use AI as their supportive partner and will heavily focus their skills, experience, and time on the people side of things (as I describe in the earlier chapter 'Projects Are About People').

And perhaps those who deliver 'projects as usual' will significantly rely on the AI aids and, because their projects are simper, smaller in scale, and less people intensive, will have no need for a project management type role.

In the AI/PM World, Will Certifications Be Valueless?

I mean, if AI is taking over 80 percent of the job, and AI does not need to be trained or certified once it is up and running and learning, then what is the purpose or value of any of the current existing certifications?

The below list is by no means a comprehensive and complete list of project management 'qualifications' out there in the big wide world of training and certification, but I am sure you get the idea; there are plenty, more than enough, and it is bloody confusing for anyone trying to make logical comparisons:

- APM Project Fundamentals Qualification (PFQ)
- APM Project Management Qualification (PMQ)
- APM Project Professional Qualification (PPQ)

- APM Project Risk Management Single Subject Certificate
- APM Earned Value Management Certification
- APM Project Planning & Control
- CIPM Certificate in Project Management
- IntroCIPM Introductory Certificate in Project Management
- CrtAgPM Certificate in Agile Project Management
- CrtAPM Certificate in Advanced Project Management
- CrtPME Project Management Essentials
- CrtPRM Certificate in Project Risk Management
- CrtEVM Earned Value Management
- CIPM-RT Certificate in PM with specialisation in Roads & Transport
- CIPM-Health Certificate in PM with specialisation in Health Care
- PM² Basic Certification
- PM² Essentials Certification
- PM² Advanced Certification
- PM² Agile Certification
- PM² Expert Certification
- PM² Trainer Certification
- CPM Certified Project Manager
- PPMC Program & Portfolio Management Certification
- PMM Program Management Mastery Advanced Certification
- CAPM Certified Associate in Project Management
- PMP Project Management Professional
- PMI-ACP PMI Agile Certified Practitioner
- PMI-PBA PMI Professional in Business Analysis
- PMI-RMP PMI Risk Management Professional
- PMI-SP PMI Scheduling Professional
- PgMP Program Management Professional
- PfMP Portfolio Management Professional
- IPMA Level D Certified Project Management Associate
- IPMA Level C Certified Project Manager
- IPMA Level B Certified Senior Project Manager
- IPMA Level A Certified Project Director
- PRINCE2 Foundation
- PRINCE2 Practitioner
- PRINCE2 Agile Foundation
- PRINCE2 Agile Practitioner
- CSM Certified Scrum Master
- A-CSM Advanced Certified ScrumMaster
- CSP-SM Certified Scrum Professional ScrumMaster
- CSPO Certified Scrum Product Owner
- A-CSPO Advanced Certified Scrum Product Owner

- CSP-PO Certified Scrum Professional Product Owner
- CSD Certified Scrum Developer
- CSP Certified Scrum Professional
- CAL Certified Agile Leadership
- CTC Certified Team Coach
- CEC Certified Enterprise Coach
- CST Certified Scrum Trainer
- CompTIA Project+
- PPM Professional in Project Management
- CPD Certified Project Director
- PSM I/II/III Professional Scrum Master
- PSPO I/II/III Professional Scrum Product Owner
- PSD I Professional Scrum Developer
- SPS Scaled Professional Scrum
- PSK I Professional Scrum with Kanban
- PAL I Professional Agile Leadership
- PSU I Professional Scrum with User Experience

Plus, it has to be acknowledged, if we are being truly honest here, that training, preparation, and certifications are a 'cash cow' of epic proportions.

It really is a money-making machine. PMI, as just one example, has (according to their August 2020 annual report) 1,600,000 certifications registered worldwide. The current fee for a PMP[2] certification test is $555 (plus $375 for a re-test if you fail the first time) so a quick extrapolation of that gives a total revenue of $888 million (OK, not everyone took their certification last year and at that fee level, but you do get my point here I'm sure).

Preparation for the PMP can vary from a low level, get a book and self-study ($50), up to a full multi-day prep course ($3,500) so just take a low-end cost of say $1,000 and multiply that against the 1.6 million certifications out there and you get a big, big number.

Interestingly, Google have entered this world with a low-cost alternative, aimed at new interest project managers, with the Google Project Management Certificate.[3]

So, there is perhaps a second 'biggish' question that we can add to this one.

How will organisations like PMI, IPMA etc. transform their certification-based revenue flows, and the associated certifications and standards themselves, in order to be relevant and of value to the individual project manager, and the market in general, in the AI-empowered project world that will be with us before you can say 'prometric testing'?

In the past, all of these certifications were process based, which will be mostly useless in the AI world of the near future as the AI technology will be handling most of these processes and will digitally laugh in the face of such formalised bodies of knowledge and certifications.

Perhaps a sign of change, or hope, is the announcement that the PMBOK[4] 7th Edition will be based on principles rather than processes and it will be much shorter than the current edition; the first declaration is encouraging and the second is bloody well needed.

And we heard from Antonio at the start of this book about Northeastern University incorporating AI into its project management curriculum, teaching project managers how to use AI to automate and improve data sets and optimise investment value from projects.

So, perhaps, there is some progress in line with the AI rise in project management.

In the AI/PM World, Will We Abandon Methodology?

Will the project management 'bodies of knowledge' exist in an AI 'cloud' of data-driven 'intelligence' rather than in the current disparate professional bodies?

Smart organisations have long moved away from methodology towards a framework for project definition and success, guiding the less experienced project managers while not constraining the more experienced project managers.

The triple constraint never made any sense in my personal experience in project management, and certainly not in an AI world of change.

Certifications like the PMP will have to dramatically evolve or be dead and buried in five to ten years. Project leaders, powered and supported by AI, will not need to know how the 'engine' works of a project.

I drive a car, a traditional internal combustion engine car, and while I do have a basic understanding of the workings of this beast (thanks to a youth experience of owning a series of pretty cheap and rubbish vehicles that needed constant fixing), I really could not explain everything that my current car does to get me from 'A' to 'B'. As a modern high-end car, it has around 100 million lines of code in its digital components alone, just one example of what I have no knowledge of, or need to have knowledge of.

You don't need to know how a car works to use it.

You don't need to know the geography of your local world to get from one place to another in an efficient way.

And, in the quite near future, you won't need to know anything at all, except how to book an autonomous vehicle or open the door on your own autonomous vehicle and give instructions as to where you want to go.

So, will this be the same for project management in the AI future, and if so, will this mean that project management 'bodies of knowledge' will no longer exist in the minds and intellectual property vaults of fee-charging professional bodies?

Will it exist instead in an AI 'cloud' of data-driven 'intelligence' that is constantly updating and improving and will be ready and accessible to all?

We are moving from a process-based environment to a data-driven model where we will use AI and machine learning, including natural language processing, to have decision making based on data and not on personal thoughts, bias, or opinions.

Such an approach will supersede methodology since it will be specific to the project, to the moment, to opportunity, to the situation, to the resources, and the risks and the impact from you and everything else.

As such, is this the beginning of the death of methodology and the method custodians?

Is this perhaps also the chance to open up the world of project management to a truly global audience with no false barriers set up to restrict and control knowledge for profit?

A nice thought.

In the AI/PM World, Are Professional Bodies Irrelevant?

If, in the AI project world, certifications and qualifications of today are deemed irrelevant, and if methodology is a thing of history in an AI-enabled project management future then what will be the role of the professional bodies or organisations?

And if community and collaboration is the proposed answer well, think again: with the rise of social (work) tools we can self-manage much of this ourselves; do we really need to be led here?

And, if the answer to my next question on the future value of project management skills is a 'yes', then what will be left for these bodies that rose up in the 20th century?

How will they stay relevant and provide real value in the AI future?

In the AI/PM World, Will Our Skills Be Devalued?

Linked to the previous 'Can anyone "do" project management in the AI-empowered project world?' question where I considered whether project management would become a lower-level skillset, and perhaps be embedded in normal day-to-day business work, then will this in turn lead to a steady de-valuation of the status and skills valuation of project managers?

Right now, project management is on the 'up'.

PMI stated in 'Project Management Job Growth and Talent Gap 2017–2027' that 'by 2027, employers will need 87.7 million individuals working in project management-oriented roles';[5] that is, a lot of project 'people'.

But will that actually be the case in the AI project world? And being 'project management oriented' does not mean that these people will have the status or position of the project managers of today, does it?

And if we see a demise in the associated value of the project management professional organisations that currently support project managers, together with a reduction in value of any certifications that they may hold, and put that against a landscape of anyone be able to lead projects (at least at the less complex business as usual level), will our current market value be significantly reduced in the AI world?

Much to Ponder

It is a lot to consider and process, I realise that, but big change is coming and by default the landscape of project management that we have today will not support this exciting future.

Exactly what this impact will look like is difficult to predict with any level of certainty but most 'experts' agree that some level of disruption is unavoidable; the Association for Project Management (APM[6]) explores this in their update to the 'Projecting the Future' report and declares:

> Project management's future: the adaptive profession – The project profession will be the profession at the heart of delivering and creating change in the years ahead and adaptability will be key.[7]

This fits precisely with the sentiment in my own book, *Make Your Business Agile: A Roadmap for Transforming Your Management and Adapting to the 'New Normal'*.

Much will have to change or be left behind as a redundant branch of evolution of our profession.

It is both scary and exciting all at once.

> Who wants change?
> 'Yes' I hear you all cry out.
> Who wants to change?
> '?' now that is the real question.
> Perhaps turn that around.
> 'Who want to not change and be left behind?'

We always overestimate the change that will occur in the next two years and underestimate the change that will occur in the next ten. Don't let yourself be lulled into inaction.

(Bill Gates[8])

Notes

1. Susie Palmer-Trew and Peter Taylor, *Project Management: It's All Bollocks!* Routledge, 2020, p. xviii.
2. Project Management Professional.
3. Google Project Management Certificate. https://grow.google/project management
4. The Project Management Body of Knowledge is a set of standard terminology and guidelines for project management. The body of knowledge evolves over time and is presented in *A Guide to the Project Management Body of Knowledge* published by PMI. The sixth edition was released in 2017 and the seventh edition is due in 2021.
5. PMI, 'Project management job growth and talent gap: 2017–2027', 2017. www.pmi.org/learning/careers/job-growth
6. The Association for Project Management promotes the professional disciplines of project management and programme management in the UK, where it is the largest professional body of its kind. APM received its Royal Charter in 2017.
7. APM, 'Projecting the future: A one-year update on the big conversation', 2020. www.apm.org.uk/media/46673/ptf_wrap_up_paper-v7-web.pdf
8. William Henry Gates III is an American business magnate, software developer, investor, author, and philanthropist. He is a co-founder of Microsoft Corporation.

Thoughts from the Real World:

> '3,000 years ago, there was no AI and the projects (e.g., pyramids) were successfully accomplished. AI is not something we ultimately need, rather it is like a car, you do not need it, but it gives you some new perspectives, opportunities, and a lot of advantages. AI is not something a project manager needs, but it will become (at some point) part of our life just like a car has become, and we definitely should make a use of it in order to make our life easier'!

Chapter 13

Survey

Introduction

I have drawn on this survey throughout this book and I appreciate the contributions and candidness from all participants.

If the statistics and figures mentioned in this chapter are of interest and use to you, then please contact me and I will happily share the full survey with you for your use in discussing and, hopefully, promoting the rise of AI in project management.

As with all such surveys, you gain insight only from how people respond and from who responds but I do believe that the number, location, and role of respondents offers a reasonably balanced view of how people feel about project management and AI.

AI in Project Management: Survey Response Details

The survey was undertaken from 1 January 2021 to 15 February 2021 (SurveyMonkey). In total, 116 respondents completed the full survey; Figure 13.1 shows their geographical representation. All major regions were represented, although with a stronger representation in Europe and North America.

There was a good range of roles in those who responded (see Figure 13.2). As expected, the majority defined their role within the 'project manager' category.

In addition to the geographical spread and good role coverage, there was a wide range of project-based experience. 'Newbie' project personnel were well represented, as were all levels of experience, although with a heavy response rate from those with over five years' experience (see Figure 13.3).

Having found out information about the respondents in this way, the survey led on to the first 'AI in project management' question, which was

DOI: 10.4324/9781003175063-13

110 Survey

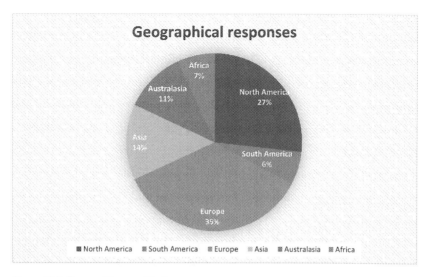

Figure 13.1 Survey: Geographical responses

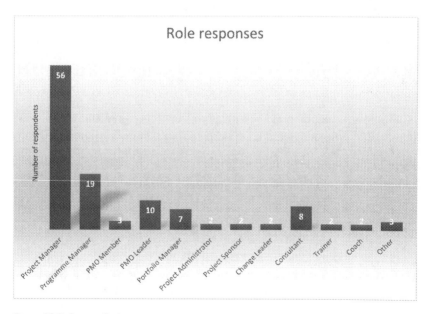

Figure 13.2 Survey: Role responses

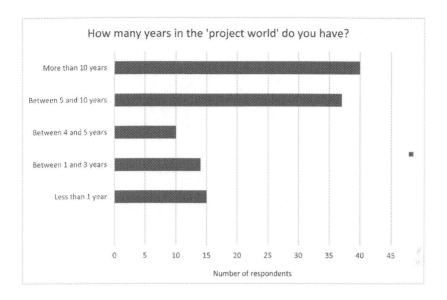

Figure 13.3 Survey: Years of experience

'How would you describe your understanding of AI (artificial intelligence) in relation to the project management profession?' (see Figure 13.4).

Interestingly, a small percentage (3 percent) felt that they were 'expert' in the subject already, while 21 percent stated that they had no knowledge or understanding of this emerging technology, and the impact it may have on their profession of project management.

Moreover, 30 percent felt they had a limited understanding and 20 percent that they had an increasing awareness of AI in project management. Just over a quarter (26 percent) considered their understanding of AI in relation to the project management profession to be 'quite good'.

So quite a mixture and range of understanding.

The second question was 'Do you already use some AI technology in your project work?' (see Figure 13.5).

Three respondents were honest enough to admit that they had no idea if their organisation was using any form of AI as yet, while a total of 68 (59 percent) declared that nothing at all was yet utilised that could be described as AI.

Moreover, 31 respondents noted limited use and 14 quite a lot of use, so 39 percent had active AI use within their company and project management work, which perhaps maps well with the previous 'How would you describe your understanding of AI (artificial intelligence) in relation

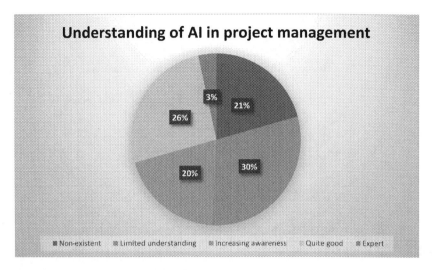

Figure 13.4 Survey: Understanding of AI

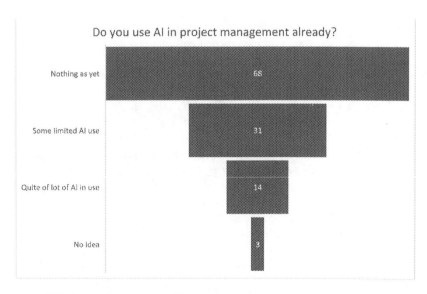

Figure 13.5 Survey: Current use of AI

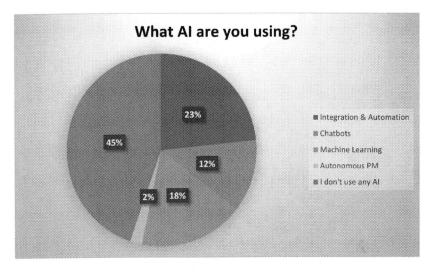

Figure 13.6 Survey: Types of AI in use

to the project management profession?' answers (3 percent expert and 26 percent quite good experience).

For the remainder of respondents, presumably the knowledge was outside of practical usage.

Focusing now on those who do use AI in project management currently (see Figure 13.6), the survey asked 'If you do use AI already, then what types of AI would you say it is' – and for this there multiple selections were possible under the headings of:

- Integration and Automation
- Chatbots
- Machine Learning
- Autonomous PM

88 respondents (45 percent) confirmed no use at all (intriguingly, this was slightly less that the 59 percent from the previous survey question).

But 55 percent (in total) were using one, or more, of the four AI categories.

Figure 13.7 focuses specifically on the responses to the following survey question: 'If you do use AI already, then what types of AI would you say it is?'

No surprises here (apart from one) as they mostly align with the development curve of AI usage, starting with the most common, (current)

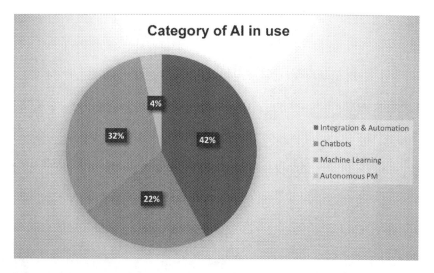

Figure 13.7 Survey: Category of AI in use

Integration and Automation at 42 percent. This is followed by Chatbots at 27 percent, then Machine Learning at 32 percent.

Perhaps the 4 percent for Autonomous PM is a result of confusion or misunderstanding of what 'autonomous' means – in its simplest sense, autonomy is about a person's ability to act on his or her own values and interests. Taken from ancient Greek, the word means 'self-legislation' or 'self-governance'.

Further, an autonomous machine or system is able to operate without being controlled directly by humans – something that, within project management certainly, is not yet possible.

Based on these levels of understanding and experience with AI in project management, the survey moved on to explore how people felt about AI in project management.

The first question in this category was 'How do you "feel" about the rise of AI in project management?' (see Figure 13.8).

A comforting small number of people felt scared by the 'rise' of AI in their profession (2 respondents) and few felt concerned (3 respondents), with the majority being somewhere between intrigued and exciting (59 and 50 respondents, respectively).

Two people, apparently, had no interest (although, it seems, enough of an interest to respond to a survey on AI in project management).

The question 'Do you personally think that AI will change project management?' aimed to understand the perceived impact that AI would have (see Figure 13.9).

Survey 115

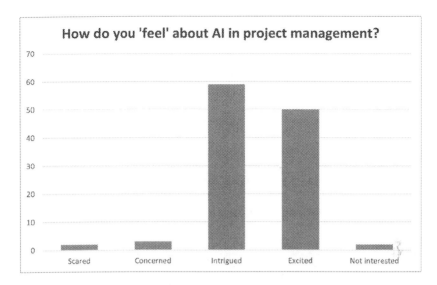

Figure 13.8 Survey: How do you 'feel' about AI in project management?

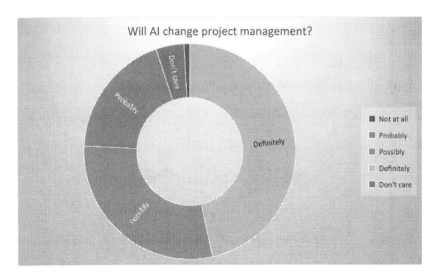

Figure 13.9 Survey: Will AI change project management?

A single respondent felt that nothing would change and that project management would go on as is right now.

Most respondents disagreed with this view.

Not at all	1
Probably	22
Possibly	34
Definitely	54
Don't care	5

Noting the five who just didn't seem to care one way or the other, the vast majority answered with a clear 'yes' to this (95 percent).

And the 'winning' belief was that AI will definitely impact project management.

The survey concluded with the question (provocative?) 'Do you think AI will eventually "end" the role of the project manager?' (see Figure 13.10).

78 percent felt that there is still a future for project managers (and project management).

A small percentage (3 percent) believed that AI would indeed (eventually) remove the need and role of the project manager, and 9 percent felt that this could possibly be the 'endgame' of the rise of AI into the world of project management.

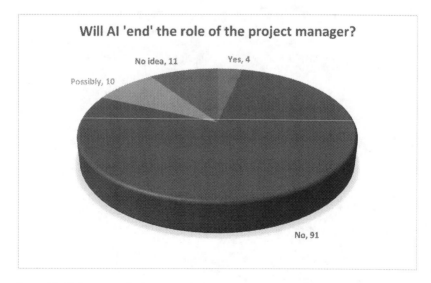

Figure 13.10 Survey: Will AI 'end' the role of the project manager?

Personal Thoughts

The following are just some examples of the comments received from survey respondents (over 100 in total were received and so the author would like to thank each and every respondent for their time). Note: I have included the name of the commentator where it was provided to me, and I am really sorry that I could not include every single comment but I did read each and every one.

The question was: 'Please share your personal thoughts on the future of project management in regard to AI'.

- AI will free up project managers from tedious duties and will help them to focus on the most relevant part of PM, working with people. AI will simplify detection of trends and health of projects. Coping with today's complexity will be made easier!
- Like any improvement there will be twists and turns before it is seen as useful, usual, and then we will wonder how we ever managed without it. *Bronwyn Kelaher.*
- According to my 2020 MSc. research on the 'Application of AI for Construction Project Planning', it was discovered that 80 percent of project managers claim their organisations have no current business strategy for dealing with upcoming AI advancements and Cost Estimating, Scheduling and Information Management are ranked as the top three project management areas that could be made more efficient using AI. I believe the potential for AI disrupting the project management methodology is already imminent, but this has not been fully explored to a meaningful extent, most organisations have not defined an AI strategy, and this will be important in the successful incorporation of AI and ultimately, the delivery of project success in the future. *Oghenemaro Louis Sota.*
- It would be good if AI took charge of planning and monitoring activities such as identifying tasks, their order, the estimates, and resource allocation for example. Tracking costs and capturing progress and reporting too can be done by AI. The value of AI carrying out these functional means that the Project Manager has time to focus the 'human-side' such as using Emotional Intelligence for team collaboration and communication. The human touch must not be lost. The PM can focus more on serving/leading the team instead of managing all the data collection and documentation, which may be seen as 'mundane' tasks. Perhaps AI can present calculated decision option variables, but the PM should make the final choice. *Bina Champaneria.*
- Integrating time, cost, and scope elements to iterate new project scenarios. *Yazan Darwazeh.*

- We really don't actually have a choice in this, it is not a 'take it or leave' option. AI is coming!
- It is way too early to be thinking about the application of artificial intelligence into the project management world.
- Project management is a dying need in most organisations, so AI is either irrelevant or the replacement to project management.
- AI in some form has been the result of a project creating business intelligence to create efficiency and value in the form of automation and business intelligence. AI for future project management will be designed to deliver measurable insight into cost, benefit, and risk based on past project scope team roles and formations. The right practitioner will use AI as a tool to predict outcomes, select the team, and execute the human activities that deliver results.
- I think that AI could play a huge role in Project Management in reducing the number of administrative tasks that Project Managers are often required to do. This reduction will pave the way for them to be able to add value in other areas, away from checking tasks of a list and scheduling meetings. *Kieran O'Driscoll.*
- Project Manager can't be replaced by AI in the next 10 years.
- Some companies are still so confused on project management … cumbersome and technical debt stand in way of use of AI, but it just needs to start.
- Building relationships and genuine and authentic relationships… will AI be able to top that human skill?
- AI will revolutionise the areas of project management requiring high human intervention, specially those tasks that consist redundant decision making. All professionals should brace for the impact AI will bring to project management and prepare themselves accordingly before the industry is disrupted and their methodologies become obsolete. *Adnan Raees Abbasi.*
- AI is just yet another smoke screen on project management incompetence.
- Artificial Intelligence (AI) is definitely the way forward and Project Management will also benefit out of it. As Project Managers, we should be open to the change (like change management during our projects) and see the brighter side of things AI will bring in our day-to-day functioning of projects. As it is said 'Change is the new constant'. *Ashish Lahori.*
- Project Management is all about leading people towards pre-defined goals. AI will not be capable of leading people in any foreseeable future. However, AI has a clearly a role in supporting Project and Programme Managers, by producing and assessing management information, undertaking repetitive tasks, and avoiding systematic errors. *Ricardo Santos.*

- I can only believe that AI will be a bonus for every serious project manager out there; these are exciting times.
- AI will transform the role of PM from implementer to business transformation and business enablement agent. PM will become closer to business. *Mashhood Ahmed.*
- Not yet prepared for the discussion! Show me first!
- AI will revolutionise Project Management, creating opportunities for automation of simple processes/tasks/activities and redirecting people (Project Managers / teams) to focus on the things that matter and require the human touch. AI is an enabler, not a replacement.
- NLP and ML Tech that enables bringing in past project information and hence assisting in planning and monitoring is my wish. *Rajan HV.*
- Large portions of this technology will be deployed in the next 1–2 years on the basis of cost-cutting initiatives. Challenges and realization of the true potential will come later.
- I think the idea of using AI for Project Management is exciting. The possibilities of having 'intelligence' help us with providing information that is more non-emotion based. Getting a schedule that works right for a team takes a lot of effort, and there are so many external factors. If the Project Manager could have this help and just focus on more of the 'people' stuff that would be fantastic.
- As a PM I am communicating with people all the time. Sometimes I need just to listen to them or give advice, award someone or downgrade others, I need to handle with conflict situation or just to bring chocolate to someone who is desperate. No AI could do that when it comes to people. *Joana Zlateva.*
- Machines can predict and analyse but cannot replace humans where emotional, empathetical and human touch is required. *Gaurang Vora.*
- AI will definitely add value to project management, especially in automating some of the more repetitive tasks. But for AI to be really be a game changes in project management, it will require accurate and diligent collection by PMs as training data.
- Project management has, and always will, shape its own future. If the people want AI, the people will get AI. If the powers don't want it, then it will be sidelined for as long as possible to protect the status quo.
- One of the most important responsibilities for the project manager is to be a manager of people. With WFH (working from home) and remote teams, this is even more important. That aspect of project management can never (I believe) be replaced by any sort of AI. *Tim Damgaard Christensen.*
- In terms of decision making, AI has been within project planning for some time. What-if scenarios are a part of everyday life for any

project team. We have had tools at our fingertips for many years to offset and mitigate project issues. Critical chains and risk management enable us to make decisions based on many factors. To automate this and delegate the decision process to machine intelligence is more than real. However, where critical decisions are needed, either fiscal or safety, human intervention is the only option at this time. To allow AI to make this kind of decision would expose PMs to litigation or personal prosecution if the decision ended up a poor one! Delegation of authority would be a difficult area; how can you prescribe to an AI outcome if you know it is wrong but don't have the authority to overturn? This is a fascinating area and one that could change the face of projects as we know them. *Terry Redmond.*

- I am intrigued at the potential of AI in project management but welcome any automated process that will help reduce the manual legwork of project personnel to manage, control, monitor, evaluate, and report on portfolio, programme, and project progression. *Andy P Jordan.*
- The nature of people and workgroups seems to create a permanent need for project managers to organize their good intentions and keep people and teams moving forward. *David Mullaney.*
- AI is great feature and as a project manager in the fintech, we encounter a lot of AI projects that require we imbibe the same concepts in our projects. I am very delighted about the new book and I am positive AI will go along helping PM.
- In my over 30 years in Project Management there have not been many surprises, but I am definitely intrigued to see how PMs can use AI in a similar manner as other areas to automate manual repetitive processes (such as Status reports) and free up time for the PM to focus on human required tasks. Looking forward to your book! *John Girton.*
- AI will improve the quality of products in our future. We should definitely be excited about it and willing to learn to deal with our new 'teammate'. *Jens Riester.*
- I believe the biggest challenge/gap is demystifying what all falls under this umbrella of AI. One question above alludes to many of the areas. But I personally feel that many of our Project Managers have no idea what those things are... or could be. *Rich Weller.*
- We are already 'behind the curve' on understanding what AI can do for project management.
- The topic itself is too new ... No discussions, no open questions, no evidence. A lot to do – if you are serious. *Evgeny Ravich.*
- AI will only add to laziness, clumsiness, and poor project performance. The difference between good and bad project managers is the ability to identify and seize opportunity. Opportunities are rarely

linked to directly to issues; it is the synergy that the human will notice.
- AI will make some things easy and will automate routine tasks – but it will not solve dilemmas and it will not replace a human any time soon.
- It will be curious to see how AI in project management will relate (if at all) with client AI systems. I am referring in particular to development management/technical assistance projects. For example, projects in support of AI in judiciary and/or donors assistance coordination. *Oxana Gutu.*
- Project Management definitely needs Intelligence. Be it Natural or Artificial. *Arun Rammohan.*
- Quality attendance to the human dimensions of change is so much more important. How can we transform our projects into meaningful and inspirational human stories of impact? How can we consistently leverage emotional intelligence to connect and enliven our stakeholders and inform our governance? How can we preference pragmatism and behavioural acuity over unchanging systems and process? AI may have its place for analytics – but it is only as good as the human inputs it receives. As with all tooling, let's get the fundamentals right before grabbing a shiny object/system/software that may end up subduing those important instincts. *Martin Parlett.*
- 3,000 years ago, there was no AI and the projects (e.g., pyramids) were successfully accomplished. AI is not something we ultimately need, rather it is like a car, you do not need it, but it gives you some new perspectives, opportunities, and a lot of advantages. AI is not something a project manager needs, but it will become (at some point) part of our life just like a car has become, and we definitely should make a use of it in order to make our life easier!

Chapter 14

A Final Word
Fish Have Hands

Someone mentioned *Terminator*, someone mentioned *Skynet*, so I thought why not, why not go down this line for when I first heard the term 'artificial intelligence'.

And I am sure the reality is that most of you, at some point, had the same thought, albeit briefly – but, of course, we don't really think that we're about to launch into the Terminator Skynet world at all when it comes to AI.

Let me give you a great example as to why that is highly unlikely (certainly in my lifetime).

Two opposing and challenging experiences in the AI world.

On one side you have got the UK Patent Office. The UK Patent Office[1] is one of the oldest, or longest continuous, patent offices or traditions in the world, actually. It's one of those weird things where it's really hard to find out which one was first out there, but the UK one has been going since the 15th century so it's quite established and could easily have been the first one.

In 1449, Henry VI of England granted the earliest known English patent for invention to Flemish-born John of Utynam through an open letter marked with the King's Great Seal called a Letter Patent. It gave John a 20-year monopoly of making stained glass for Eton and this was used in Eton College amongst other places.

Now, why is this important as far as an AI conversation goes? Well, a lady called Kathy Barra pointed me in this direction, because there has already been a case of an AI patent application: it's known as the Davis hearing decision, where someone attempted to lodge a patent, that was created, or invented by AI.

Let that sink in for a while.

The argument was that this non-human entity (thing, whatever word you should be using here) had invented something – I don't know what it was actually – but it was created, it was invented, and there was a patent application, and the origin of it was AI.

DOI: 10.4324/9781003175063-14

Now, the actual decision that came down as a result of this was that you cannot have a patent or an invention that has been created by a non-human at this point in time. But the UK Patent Office has already said that while this application was rejected, there should be a debate for the future because this is something that needs to be considered and addressed within the near future.

On the other hand, there is a great TED talk by Janelle Shane,[2] and she is talking about how weird AI is right now.[3]

'The danger of artificial intelligence isn't that it's going to rebel against us, but that it's going to do exactly what we ask it to do.'

Check out the TED talk, because AI researcher Janelle Shane shares the weird, sometimes alarming, antics of AI algorithms as they try to solve human problems – like creating new ice cream flavours or recognising cars on the road. Here is the one about why fish have hands.

One AI programme has been unable to understand the concept of a hand and the fish in the sense that they are different, separate in fact. It believes that human fingers and the fish are one thing on the grounds that most of the images that it presumably has consumed are of people holding fish, and therefore right now, it cannot differentiate between the two (fishermen of the world you have a lot to answer for here).

Well, there you have it; you have got the two extremes there that is AI in its very early days but obviously alongside that the thoughts for the very near future.

This is something that we need to really think about. And it will undoubtedly change how projects are delivered and how project management as a practice will evolve.

The true reality is that this is inevitable; there is no fighting it, there is no resistance to it, it will come to pass, and you will have to change, adapt, or go find something else to do with your life.

Personally, I was delighted to have this opportunity to explore AI in the world of project management, and I remain positive that it will be a huge benefit to the profession.

There is an exciting future for project managers: independent thinking – creative – compassionate – collaborative – and even more successful than today, powered by AI and focused on people.

Peter

Notes

1 The Intellectual Property Office (IPO) is the official UK government body responsible for intellectual property (IP) rights including patents, designs, trademarks, and copyright. IPO is an executive agency, sponsored by the Department for Business, Energy & Industrial Strategy,

2 Janelle Shane is an optics research scientist and AI researcher, writer, and public speaker. She keeps a popular science blog called *AI Weirdness*, where she documents various machine learning algorithms, both ones submitted by readers and ones she personally creates.
3 Janelle Shane, 'The danger of AI is weirder than you think'. TED talk, 2019. www.ted.com/talks/janelle_shane_the_danger_of_ai_is_weirder_than_you_think?language=en

Chapter 15

Other Weird and Interesting Facts

This is such an exciting, fast-developing topic that you can find incredible stories and facts about what artificial intelligence (AI) can do, and what it can't (fish with hands, say no more).

Here are just a few that I came across while researching for this book that I just could not resist sharing.

Enjoy:

- Sophia, a lifelike humanoid, has gained guaranteed citizenship of Saudi Arabia. This has brought much controversy as the public wonders and questions whether or not robots should have rights.
- Most BOTS are female – if you ask Siri, Alexa, Cortana, or your bank's Voice assistance a question, most likely, you will be answered by a pleasant and polite woman's voice. The reason? Studies show that males and females are more attracted to a woman's voice.
- AI can read your mind. Scary, right? A new methodology has been developed by roboticists that can create an image of your thoughts using an FMRI scanner. The AI is designed to construct an image from your brain and compare it with other pictures, received from volunteers.
- AI recognises emotions. A robot built in the late 1990s called Kismet can recognise emotions through human body language and voice tone.
- AI can write. A robot wrote an article on an earthquake in California on the *Los Angeles Times* website, gathering data from a seismograph. Another example is *Harry Potter and the Portrait of What Looked Like a Large Pile of Ash*, which is the title of a Potter novel written by AI. Botnik Studios, a comic writing enterprise that uses machines to make content, created an algorithm that learned to write based on J.K. Rowling's books. And while the three chapters that you can get acquainted with online

DOI: 10.4324/9781003175063-15

probably will not bring you as much pleasure as the original, they are key to understanding the logic of AI.

Tianhe-2, or the 'Milky Way 2', is a supercomputer located in the National Supercomputer Center in Guangzhou, China. Developed by a team of 1,300 scientists and engineers, it is capable of physics-related applications.

IBM's Project Debater showed us that AI can even be successful at debating humans in complex subjects. Not only is it able to research a topic, but it can also create an engaging point of view and craft rebuttals against a human opponent.

In 2016, Alex Da Kid released the song 'Not Easy', which reached number four on the iTunes charts within 48 hours. What made this song unusual was that it was produced in collaboration with IBM, who had their Watson BEAT system analyse five years' worth of data to find a significant cultural theme that Alex could use in his song. With Watson's devised theme of heartbreak as Alex's inspiration, the AI then analysed the beats, rhythms, and melodies of popular songs, giving the songwriter a better idea of how the song should sound. Alex Da Kid, already being a successful music producer, then had ample material to create an instant hit.

And, if you want to have some fun, try these out:

Picture: You now create terrible drawings and let Google guess what they are! Google released a free online game built using machine learning. It is simple, really: draw an object, and Google will attempt to guess what it is. The model only gets better with the more drawings it guesses, and all the data is shared publicly to help advance machine learning research. Play the game for yourself: https://quickdraw.withgoogle.com/

Words: Also created by Google, Semantris is a set of online word association games powered by machine-learned, natural language understanding (NLP) technology. Each time you enter a clue, the model looks at the words in play and selects the one it thinks is most related. The model learned the connections between words after being fed billions of conversational text samples on the internet. Try it for yourself: https://research.google.com/semantris/

My Valued Contributors

As usual, I have relied heavily on people who just know more than me to provide the real detail and inspiration in this book.

You can read all of their amazing profiles below, and I urge you to connect to them all and talk with them in their various areas of expertise.

Antonio Nieto-Rodriguez

Antonio Nieto-Rodriguez is the global champion of project management. He has transformed project management into one of the central issues on every CEO's 2030 agenda. He is the creator of concepts such as the 'Hierarchy of Purpose' featured in the *Harvard Business Review*, or the 'Project Economy', which argues that projects are the lingua franca of the business and personal worlds from the C-suite to managing your career.

Antonio's research and global impact in modern management has been recognised by Thinkers50 with the prestigious award 'Ideas into Practice' and he is ranked #17 in the global gurus Top 30 list. He is part of Marshall Goldsmith 100 coaches.

He was the global Chairman of the Project Management Institute in 2016. He is the Founder of Projects & Co and the Co-founder of the Brightline Initiative and the Strategy Implementation Institute. He is the Director of the Programme Management Office at GlaxoSmithKline Vaccines. Previously, he worked as Head of Project Portfolio Management at BNP Paribas Fortis. Prior to this he was Head of Post-Merger Integration at Fortis Bank, leading the acquisition of ABN AMBRO, the largest in financial service history. He also worked for ten years at PricewaterhouseCoopers, becoming the global lead practitioner for project and change management. Antonio is currently Visiting Professor at Duke CE, Instituto de Empresa, Solvay, Vlerick, and Skolkovo.

His work focuses on advising senior leaders on how to lead transformational change; prioritise and implement strategic initiatives; build high-performing teams; and work across silos and become a learning organisation – all essential elements to create a culture that strives for execution, excellence, and collaboration.

Antonio is the author of *Lead Successful Projects* (Penguin, 2019), *The Project Revolution* (LID, 2019), and *The Focused Organization* (Taylor & Francis, 2014); he is currently writing the *HBR Project Management Handbook* (expected September 2021) and has contributed to seven other books.

He is a much-in-demand speaker at events worldwide. Antonio has presented at more than 300 conferences around the world, regularly evaluated as the best speaker. Some of the events where he has delivered inspirational keynotes include the European Business Summit, Strategy Leaders Forum, Gartner, Fail, TEDx, and EU Cohesion Conference.

Born in Madrid, Spain, and educated in Germany, Mexico, Italy, and the United States, Antonio is fluent in five languages. He is an economist, has an MBA from London Business School and Insead's IDP.

Craig Mackay

Craig Mackay is the Co-founder and CEO at Sharktower.

With over 20 years' experience in large-scale programme and transformation delivery working at all levels across project development, implementation, PMO, assurance, and programme director roles, Craig knows only too well the challenges faced in delivering change but also knows how wasteful project management practices have become.

Craig went on to co-found the AI-driven project management software company Sharktower, with a deep belief that businesses can make better decisions, align people better around required outcomes, remove wasted manual effort, and ultimately increase the likelihood of success outcomes if project delivery is more data driven.

Bentzy Goldman

Bentzy is the Founder of Perflo, an innovative start-up that helps project teams and their organisations to measure and increase performance through the use of cutting-edge research and technology.

He is extremely passionate about all things 'future of work' and dreams of a world where Monday mornings are looked forward to, not resented.

www.perflo.co: Project Team Performance Analytics. The new way to measure performance and increase alignment in your project-based teams.

Lee Lambert

In the profession of project management, Lee R. Lambert, PMP, PMI Fellow, has established the standard against which others in the field are measured.

Throughout a fast-paced 18-year corporate career with Chicago Bridge & Iron, Lawrence Livermore National Laboratory, General Electric (Nuclear Reactor Division), and Battelle Memorial Institute – where he worked almost exclusively with engineers and scientists – he quickly ascended to senior management positions and was responsible for the development and implementation of ground-breaking, sophisticated Enterprise project management processes for engineering, medical diagnostics, and research and development.

In 1981, as a result of his pragmatic application of project management methodologies, he was invited to be an integral part of the creation of the Project Management Institute's (PMI) Project Management Professional (PMP) Certification Programme. He is a recipient of the PMI's Distinguished Contribution Award and was a member of the PMNetwork/PM Journal Editorial Review team for over a decade. He also contributed as a Subject Matter Expert (SME) to the PMI's Earned Value Management System (EVMS) Practice Standard.

Educated as a mechanical engineer, he is a holder of a Master's Certificate in Project Management from George Washington University. Lambert is a frequent lecturer in the prestigious Washington University's Executive Roundtable series. His most recent professional recognition was being named as one of only 70 PMI Fellows. He also received one of the PMI's highest honours for his ground-breaking applied learning programmes: The Professional Development Provider of the Year 2007.

As an author of two books and 32 professional papers, no other project management educator/speaker can contend with his uncanny technical knowledge, material content, and refreshing and entertaining delivery – his hard-hitting but humorous style has mesmerised more than 50,000 students in 23 countries. He is now partnering with Roeder Consulting, Inc. to continue his excellent work.

Lee takes the saying; 'Been there, done that, got the T-shirt' to a new level.

Marco Steidel

Marco Steidel, MSc, PMP, PMI-ACP, PRINCE2, PSM-I, SAFe, is an experienced senior IT consultant and project manager with more than 15 years' professional experience in various industries.

Apart from duties in the project management office, his focus is on classical and agile project management in the environment of global IT outsourcing projects with high demand for automation, cost control, and IT security. His passion is to mediate between the classical predictive way and the agile world of project management, as well as to promote the digitalisation of individual work steps that serve the project manager's work and ensure project success.

Besides his interest and contribution to project management as a project manager and PM-consultant, Marco is a creative thinker and leader in helping clients in optimising their IT infrastructure and fostering digital transformation through providing consulting in the fields of IT strategy, cybersecurity, business development, and digital business model innovation.

One last time, thank you...

A last thought from the Future Real World:

'Artificial intelligence will reach human levels by around 2029.

Follow that out further to, say, 2045, we will have multiplied the intelligence, the human biological machine intelligence of our civilization a billion-fold'.

(Ray Kurzweil)

I'll Be Back

I just couldn't resist it, sorry.

'I'll be back', in 2022, with a ground-breaking book titled *Project Team Performance Management*, which will also be published by Routledge.

Hasta la vista readers!

Index

Abbasi, A 118
Accenture 9
Adams, D 55, 61
Ahmed, M 119
'AI Winter' 12
Alex Da Kid 126
Alexa 5, 125
AlphaGo 14, 15
Amazon 25, 30
association of project management (APM) 22, 106
applied intelligence 6
artificial general intelligence (AGI) 6, 42
artificial intelligence 101 5
artificial narrow intelligence (ANI) 5, 29
Austin, T 80, 85
autonomous project manager 18, 113

Barker, J 26
Barra, K 122
Berners-Lee, T 13, 15
Bokman, A 53
Boudreau, P 1, 20, 22, 91, 96
Brady, T 69
Brown, D 1
Burger, R 80, 85

Capek, K 12, 15
CERN 13, 15
Champaneria, B 117
chatbots 17–18, 113
Christensen, D 119
Clifford, C 9
The Coffee Test 19
computer vision 6

Cora PPM 84, 85
Cortana 5, 18, 125
COVID-19 7, 14, 94

dark data 7
Darwazeh, Y 117
Dastin, J 39
data-driven 'intelligence' 103
Davies, A 69
The Davis hearing decision 122
deep learning 6
DeepMind 14, 15, 22
Descartes, R 12, 15
digital native 87–88
Drucker, P 79, 85

Einstein, A 32, 39
The Employment Test 19
Eugene Goostman (computer/chatbot) 15, 20
earned value management system (EVMS) 78, 83, 85
explainable artificial intelligence (XAI) 25, 27–29

Feigelbinder, M 20, 22
Forbes 7

general artificial intelligence (GAI) 29
Gartner 7, 65
Gates, W 106
generation alpha 96
Girton, J 120
Goertzel, B 19, 22
Goldman, B 41, 128
Google 102, 106
Google Assistant 5

Index

Google Picture 126
Goostman, E 13, 15
generative pre-trained transformer 3 (GPT-3) 42
Gutu, O 121

Hawking, S 8
Heinlein, R 75
Hephaestus 11
Heraclitus 87, 95
Hesiod 11, 14
Hitchhiker's Guide to the Galaxy 55
Hung, M 80, 85
HV, Rajan 119

international atomic energy agency (IAEA) 94
IBM Deep Blue 13–15, 78, 84–85
IBM Project Debater 126
IBM Watson 13, 15
IBM Watson BEAT 126
integration and automation 18, 113
Intellectual Property Office 123
intelligent automation 6
International project management association (IPMA) 60–61, 102
iTunes 126

Jordan, A 120

Kaniouram, A 7
Kasparov, G 13–16, 78
Kelaher, B 117
key performance indicator (KPI) 92, 96
Kismet 125
KISS 72, 74
'The Knowledge' 72, 74
KPMG 26, 39
Kryryliuk, A 1
Kurzweil, R 1, 132

Lahmann, M 19
Lahori, A 118
Lambert, L 77, 129
The Lazy Project Manager 52, 71, 74
lean management 96
Lewis, C 60
Luzhanskiy, I 1

machine learning 6, 18, 25, 49, 113
Mackay, C 25, 128

Make your Business Agile 105
Martin, P 80, 85
Mayor, A 11, 14
McCarthy, J 5, 13
McKinsey Global Institute 50, 53
Metropolis 41, 52
'Milky Way 2' 126
millennials 95
Mullaney, D 120

Nadella, S 53
Nieto-Rodriguez, A 103, 127
Nightingale, P 69
Nilsson, N 19, 22
Niranjan, A 22
natural language porcessing (NLP) 6, 18, 53
Norvig, P 8

O'Driscoll, K 118
organisational network analysis (ONA) 50, 53

Palmer-Trew, S 67, 69, 106
Pandora 11
Parlett, M 68, 121
Perflo 41, 52, 128
Perrey, J 53
Pichai, S 9
Pickersgill, A 53
Pink, D 66, 69
performance measurement baseline (PMB) 80, 85
project management body of knowledge (PMBOK) 103, 106
project management institute (PMI) 9, 53, 59, 60–61, 79, 85, 102, 105–106
project management office (PMO) 48–50, 53, 63–64
project management professional (PMP) 102
project management technology quotient (PMTQ) 60
Porter, D 67
project portfolio management (PPM) 53
Prashara, S 7
predictive analytics 6
process automation 17
Project Management: It's all Bollocks! 100

Project Team Performance Management 69, 133
PWC 19, 22, 47, 53, 58, 61

Rag 'n' Bone Man 32, 39
Rammohan, A 121
Ravick, E 120
Redmond, T 120
responsible AI 6
Reuters 25
Riester, J 120
robot 12, 15, 125
The Robot College Student Test 19
robotic process automation (RPA) 30
Russell, S 8

Santos, R 118
Schmelzer, R 7
Semantris 126
Shane, J 123–124
Sharktower 25, 39, 67–60, 128
Silver, N 39
Sinek, S 26, 39
Siri 5, 18, 125
Skynet 122
Smoley's Parallel Tables of Logarithms and Squares 77, 85
The Social Project Manager 66
Sophia (humanoid) 125
Sota, O 117
2001: A Space Odyssey 5
Steidel, M 87, 129

Stewart, J 53
Stobierski, T 59, 61
Sunstein, C 53
Swift, J 12, 15

Talos 11
Taylor, P 53, 69, 106
TED Conferences LLC (Technology, Entertainment, Design) 123
The Terminator 5, 41, 52, 122
Thaler, R 53
Tianhe-2 (supercomputer) 126
Truzzi, C 67
Turing, A 5, 19
The Turing Test 13, 15, 20, 22

UK Patent Office 122

Vogon 55

Walenta, T 69
Waze 73, 75
Weller, R 120
Wezenbaum, J 13, 15
Wilk, J 53
Wozniak, S 19–12, 22

Yudlowsky, E 25, 39

Zerega, B 22
Zeus 11
Zlateva, J 119

Printed in the United States
by Baker & Taylor Publisher Services